CONTENTS

Image Section

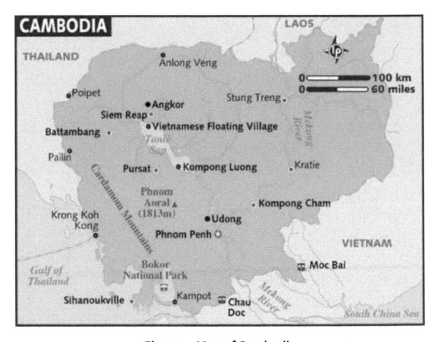

Figure 1: Map of Cambodia
('Reproduced with permission from the Lonely Planet website
www.lonelyplanet.com © 2011 Lonely Planet.)

INTRODUCTION

I first knew Addheka as my language teacher – a voice on the other end of a Skype partnership over 12 months. I had decided to learn the local Khmer language so I could better get to know the Cambodian villagers my wife and I were helping to build houses for.

When I met Addheka in Phnom Penh I noticed she was in a wheelchair but didn't probe further. As we spent more time together, our lessons often drifted off-task as I asked her about her life. My curiosity was aroused when it became clear she had both survived the Khmer Rouge regime and been disabled since she was two years old. There was also an aid project her school seemed to be involved with.

A year later I was studying with her at the KSL (Khmer School of Language) in Phnom Penh and we came to know more about each other. Once or twice we had to take a break, as her emotions overwhelmed her when reflecting on her life as a disabled person and things that might have been.

At some point I remarked that she should write her story. She told me she already had - thanks to enforced idleness when she broke her leg in 2009 - but turning this into a book would require some assistance. Was I interested in helping her with this endeavour?

Over the next 18 months we spent many hours talking, mainly online using Skype but also in Cambodia, where we visited the places that held her story. We went to the flat rice fields of Cha Huoy, to the banks of the Mekong River in Prek Eng and to the pagoda in Touk Meas where her family still remembers those departed. She introduced me to many of the people with whom she has crafted a life after the unimaginable horrors they all lived through under Pol Pot and the Khmer Rouge.

The most crucial moment in the story of this book came when Addheka told her older sister, Wantha, who is ten years older, that she was writing the story of their lives. I learnt that these two Cambodian women, so close for so long, had barely talked about the Pol Pot times since the nightmare ended. Addheka did not know if Wantha would approve of their story being told.

There was more to this than having to re-live the suffering and loss under the Khmer Rouge regime, though that was significant enough. There were skeletons in the family cupboard and Addheka was going to reveal them. In turn, this could have an effect on the other family members who had also survived the Khmer Rouge and were still alive.

Wantha gave the project her blessing, knowing that it was her younger sister's deep desire to share her remarkable and inspiring story with anyone who was interested. Reluctantly initially, Wantha allowed herself to be quizzed by me on details that Addheka either did not know about or had hazy memories of.

Seurn, an older cousin and dear friend of the two women, also allowed himself to share some details of Addheka's story. For all three, the past is so painful to recall, the losses so profound. It is my great hope that in some way their involvement in this project may prove to be cathartic.

Addheka also introduced me to some of the 600 children and their families from all over the country that she helps. The selfless, hands-on support she provides each weekend is a testament to the depth of her spiritual beliefs and sense of purpose. She has done this for nearly two decades.

Jim Pollock,
co-editor December 2015

PREFACE

I often describe my life as being of three parts. My first life was full of family and connections to life around my home in Phnom Penh. I was one of 25 full and half siblings, a testament to a father whose ambition spawned three families. Growing up I knew nothing else and never wanted for company.

I couldn't walk until I was 13 years old as I contracted polio at the age of two. School for me was something to savour, and just to be there was all I asked. I could read better than most of my peers so I knew this thing called education was going to be part of my world.

My first life, with parents, love, learning and freedom ended on 17 April 1975 with the takeover by the communist Khmer Rouge regime, led by its brutal, secretive leader, Pol Pot.

As we trudged out of Phnom Penh, herded along by the young, hate-filled, rifle- toting militants, I had no idea what was about to happen. A darkness descended on our lives that extinguished everything that made life worth living. My life spiraled downwards into isolation and depravity I could never have imagined possible, let alone one that I could survive. While those around me starved to death or succumbed to malaria or dysentery, I continued to see another sunrise.

In the darkest days and nights, my life could have been snuffed out without anyone noticing or caring. When the regime was swept away four years later, most found it hard to believe I had survived. How could a naïve, crippled child who had known only comfort and dependence, outlive almost her entire family?

Those of my family who survived have an unbreakable bond with each other. I renew their fellowship regularly and have never lived far from them. I look after them and they look after me.

Some of my family would not leave in the desperate days following the demise of the Pol Pot regime because of me. My immobility made it impossible for them to consider risking flight. That is a cross I bear, as perhaps life may have been better for them if they had left me behind and fled then.

Since that time the greatest sadness in my life is that I cannot give back to the members of my family whose lives were lost during this period, and repay their love and care. So I find other ways to give back - to show that the world is a better place for my survival, and it was not an oversight that I am still here. I care for those who need me.

I have over 600 children from very poor families who look to me when life becomes impossible. Together with the staff from the Khmer School of Language and my family members, young and old, they form the fabric of my life.

Seng BouAddheka,
December 2015

PART 1
MY FIRST LIFE

My family, taken in March 1975, from left to right: Rathya, Laddha (me),
Nora, Chittra, Ratana, Wantha, Vanna, with her two sons, Kaddeka
(standing) and Karuna, in her mother's arms. Sitting, Pan SutChay,
my mother and Seng Bou, my father.

1

TOUK MEAS, LAND OF MY GRANDFATHERS

THE MEKONG River flows some 4,300 kilometres from the highlands of China, to the flat, muddy flood plain of Vietnam and southeast Cambodia. This huge river, bringing cubic kilometres of water each year, has created a fertile landscape, depositing silt and sand as it disgorges its load into the South China Sea. Some of this land, mostly in Vietnam, is so low it is threatened by rising sea levels and may be under water in decades to come.

On the edge of this flood plain, bordering Vietnam lies the Cambodian province of Kampot. The most easterly district in Kampot province is called Banteay Meas and the random, rocky geological protrusions that jut hundreds of metres out of the surrounding flood plain, reveal we are now on higher land.

The main town in this district is called Touk Meas, and it sits on the edge of a small river, overlooked by one of the steep, rocky, heavily vegetated protrusions. In this picturesque colonial and provincial setting my parents met, some 75 years ago.

In the late 1940s Touk Meas was a small town with an administrator called Naow Pan. He was my grandfather. He had arrived on a promotion, a few years earlier, from Battambang. Pan had proved his worth in the northwest province as an administrator, and was recognised for this by being asked by the French authorities to administer the district of Banteay Meas. His family lived in government accommodation, close to the main road north to Phnom Penh.

My mother, SutChay, lived here with her much loved father Naow Pan and various full and half siblings. Her mother, Naow Pan's wife, had died when she was five and she and her three brothers now shared their home with a growing family. Pan had taken a new partner - they never married - called Yaem, and three more children were added from this relationship. SutChay was encouraged to take education seriously which she did, finding an aptitude for languages. She spoke Thai fluently from an early age, something she picked up in Battambang, where she taught as a teacher in primary schools when she was quite young.

In 1941, Japan occupied Cambodia but allowed the Vichy (pro Nazi) French to stay in charge. The French lost a small, armed conflict with Thailand, following which they handed the Cambodian provinces of Battambang and Siem Reap over as spoils to the victors. This infuriated the Cambodians who have always seen their country eaten away by the 'giants' on either side – Thailand to the west and Vietnam to the east.

A few hundred metres away from where Mother lived, there was a wealthy family by the name of Seng. Of Chinese heritage, Long Seng, my other (paternal) grandfather, had built up his wealth as a successful landowner, farming the productive land he owned near the river. The Seng family had five children, the youngest of which was my father, Seng Bou.

While both my parents spent their formative years in reasonable comfort and gained a primary school education, this relatively good life was not to last. Both families, for different reasons, crashed financially.

Most successful traders in the region were Chinese, and Long Seng had moved his wealth into setting up a rice trading business. In the mid 1940's, he became bankrupt, forcing the family to sell the land and property that had produced the wealth, including the family home. His health deteriorated after that and he soon passed away. Bou now had to move in with his older sister, Hong.

My mother's father, Naow Pan, suffered at the hands of his new partner, Yaem, who had been the hired help before my grandmother died. She now moved up the social ladder, becoming the de facto wife of a district administrator.

Unfortunately Yaem had not thrown off a long term gambling addiction, and loved to play Bir Tang, a Thai card game. Now she had more money to lose, and gradually frittered away the wealth she had access to as Pan's partner.

By the time Pan finally realized the extent of the losses it was too late. His wealth, and the prestige that went with it, were gone. Like Long Seng, he could not come to terms with the losses, and became ill. He too passed away prematurely, though by then my parents were married.

My father Bou moved in with his older sister Hong when he was 15 years old. Unfortunately, Hong had married a violent and abusive drunk, who did not welcome Bou and insisted he earn his keep by selling duck eggs on the streets of Touk Meas.

Seeking a way out of this uncomfortable domestic situation Bou eventually joined the French army as a cook, where he could earn his own money, and learnt to speak French.

SutChay met and fell in love with this sharp-witted, good-looking soldier. Naow Pan approved of them getting married and they became man and wife and subsequently my parents.

We know that they bought land and a house on the southern side of the main bridge in Touk Meas, close to the main road, and near some rice fields and plantings of fruit trees. This money must have come from SutChay's side as Bou had no wealth to speak of. Naow Pan had sanctioned their marriage, knowing his daughter was marrying a man with talent and promise but nothing of substance next to his name.

In 1946, following the end of World War Two, the French returned to Indochina, and were faced with a population that had been encouraged by the Japanese to believe they could rule themselves. Japan actually pronounced Cambodia independent in 1945 but nothing came of this. In that year the Thais were convinced to return to Cambodia the provinces that the French had ceded to them in 1941.

The army that my father joined was one that was gearing up to fight the local population who wanted independence from colonial rule. Just as Ho Chi Minh started a war against the French next door in Vietnam, so some Cambodians, calling themselves *Issaraks*, did the same.

Dad had an older brother called Try. He married and had four children with his wife, who unfortunately developed liver problems and died after giving birth to her last child. On her deathbed she asked Bou and SutChay to look after her children, perhaps not trusting Try to do that.

My parents took this request seriously and, in the years ahead, played an important role in the upbringing of these children, and their children. They also continue to be part of my story.

Dad had two other sisters who both got to know French nationals, one marrying a soldier and the other marrying a young plantation manager. The plantation manager's work took them to the provinces, but he got the fright of his life when the *Issarak* guerrillas tried (unsuccessfully) to kidnap him to draw attention to their fight for independence. That was enough for him and his wife to bring forward plans to leave Cambodia and move permanently to France.

They had already purchased a block of land in Phnom Penh and, as they were leaving, asked Bou and SutChay to look after it for them. The newly weds went to the plot of land in Phnom Penh and found it to be centrally located, next to a small canal that drained the city of floodwaters. They thought the offer of this block too good an opportunity to miss so left their home in Touk Meas and moved permanently to the capital, erecting a simple wooden structure there.

Bou was going to get involved in a hotel business and SutChay was going to look for work using her language skills as a translator. And very soon after, they would have their first child.

2

THE HOUSE BY THE CANAL
AND FATHER'S THREE WIVES

WHEN CAMBODIA gained independence from France in 1953, as my parents were in Phnom Penh they were perfectly positioned to fill some of the jobs that would now fall to locals, rather than expatriate Frenchmen, or Vietnamese.

Both had significant language skills, Mum in Thai and French and Dad in French. Mum found employment in the Ministry of Information, in the External Affairs section, translating documents between Thai and Khmer. Father applied successfully for a job in the Customs department, after his business plans ran aground. Both would keep these jobs until April 1975.

With secure and well paying jobs, SutChay and Bou started a family. Vanna was their first daughter, born in 1951, followed two years later by another girl, Wantha. By the time Phalla was born - a third girl who died after only two weeks, of umbilical tetanus - Mum was becoming desperate to have a boy.

At around this time Mum and Dad became aware of a young girl who was in trouble because of her mother's perilous financial situation. A former 'Miss Cambodia', the mother had lived the high life with royalty and other rich officials in Phnom Penh high society, but had been left high and dry as a result of her gambling debts.

My father had once partly owned the nightclub "*Tek Roam, Pkar Roam*" ("Dancing water, Dancing flower") where this young girl was effectively being sold to clear her mother's debts.

"We can't let this happen, Bou," SutChay told her husband. "Maybe she can come and live with us. She can look after the children and help around the house?"

"If you want to keep working that would make sense," Dad reasoned.

It was 'win-win'. And so the girl, Lux Noem, became part of the family. Over the next ten years Noem would nurture, love and support all of the numerous children who would live with us. She would also take on another role that was to change my mother's life forever.

I HAVE a cousin called Seurn, known to us all as *bong* Seurn (*bong* means older in Khmer). Seurn was a son of my father's only brother, Try. If you remember Seurn's mother had died after delivering a fourth child and my father had promised, on her deathbed, to look after her children. Try had remarried after her death and started another family. His new wife was more concerned for her own children and had little time for Seurn and his siblings. Try did not protect his children enough, according to neighbours, and Dad was often going to Touk Meas and bringing them back to Phnom Penh.

For several years Seurn and his sister Prong shuttled between the two homes, before Dad eventually said they could stay with him permanently. And so our family absorbed Try's children.

In 1955 there was a knock at the door one evening, and there stood an attractive lady about 20 years old, with a newborn baby in her arms. She was from Oudong, a town about 50 kilometres north of Phnom Penh, and the original capital of Cambodia. Father had been working in Oudong recently and this young Mum informed both my parents that the infant in her arms was the result of a liaison between her and Dad.

Mum was shocked, and probably deeply disappointed. It was, and is, not out of character for a stereotypical Cambodian male to be promiscuous. There was now irrefutable proof that Dad was cut from that cloth, at least when he was away from home with work.

To her great credit Mum agreed to raise the little girl, called Dara, as part of the family, and did not criticise Dad.

Mum meanwhile was prepared to do whatever she could to have a son. Her world-view was formed around Buddhist concepts of right living and building merits in this life so that the next life would be a better one. She went to the local pagoda and asked monks what she could do to ensure her next child would be a son. She was given advice, which she took - praying in the temple mainly - and became pregnant shortly thereafter.

I don't know if Mum was aware of it at the time, but Cambodian Buddhist folklore has it that a child born in this way will not live a long life. In any case, Mum's next child was male, and he was born in 1956 and called Ratana. Perhaps because of this cloud hanging over his longevity, Mum worried about him and he became her favourite child.

There were now seven children (including Noem) living under our roof. Another son, Chittra was born to Mum and Dad in 1958, and another child, Nora, the year after.

Dad was obviously attracted to other women and in 1960 it became clear that this attraction was two-way. He was handsome, quick-witted, financially secure, and, it would seem, available for sexual encounters, should the opportunity arise. Mum by now had five of her own children, a successful career, and growing connections to the Phnom Penh elite. She had a husband she loved, but who, although financially supporting the family, including my cousins, was clearly not loyal or faithful to her.

If a seed of doubt and disappointment was sown with Dara's arrival, what happened next was something much more crushing. Noem, our very attractive nanny and housekeeper, and the girl Mum and Dad had rescued, was now 20-years-old, and was found to be pregnant to Dad. Mum was furious with him but had to decide how to respond.

Noem's sexual relationship with Dad was much talked about by my Mum's friends and family alike. Everyone had an opinion about what Mum should do about it. Her relatives said she should not accept it and should follow Dad to see where he went, and make trouble for his 'women'. Also she should be unfaithful to him, just to show him she could not be taken for granted.

Mum wanted none of this. Initially she was angry with Dad not Noem, whom she continued to love and welcome into the household. Then she decided to just accept it as destiny, in the Buddhist manner. If it was destiny that her husband was acting in this way, why fight it and create trouble? If two people were drawn to each other, what good would it do to try and prevent that from happening? It would still happen but just be hidden.

It was a middle path - neither spiteful in making trouble for father and his 'wives', nor self indulgent and pitying. Mum outwardly stayed strong, independent and motherly towards her children. She told relatives her life now "was for the children".

In later years I wondered what Mum would have made of the saying I read once. "It is hard to be a woman in Cambodia. You must think like a man, act like a lady, look like a young girl, and work like a horse." It became clear that while Dad may have had one family with Mum, he still had ambitions to be the patriarch of other households.

When another young socialite, the daughter of a District Chief who worked at the Royal Palace, became pregnant to Father as well, Mum must have wondered where it would all end. From this point they drifted apart. In 1960, Noem gave Bou a son called Nareth and Mum informed him that she was now pregnant again – this time with me.

I was born on the 18th of August 1961 and called Laddha, for reasons that go to the heart of Mum's Buddhist beliefs, as I will explain later. As I was crawling and learning to be a toddler, and cuddled each day by nanny Noem, the family dramas continued to escalate.

The following year two more children were born to Dad. One to Noem, a girl, Sokunteary, and one to Prom Seylo, the beautiful young protocol advisor at the Royal Palace, who gave Dad a girl called Seilakvatei.

Seylo and Noem had been classmates together previously, but their lives had diverged since then. The two women did not get along and sparks flew when they were together.

While Noem ended up as our nanny, Seylo spent her days in the Royal Palace. Her father was the Chief of District Five of Phnom Penh. Now the two young women were competing for the affections of the same man - my father.

Noem and Seylo's two girls and I were roughly the same age and we came to be treated by Dad virtually as triplets. He would always buy us identical birthday presents, so no one could claim they were favoured.

In 1963 Mum had her last child, a boy, Rathya, with whom I spent my most precious times as a child. Rathya was two years younger than me, and the only one of my full siblings I could boss around. Despite this big-sister treatment, Rathya became my play partner, my friend, and my soul mate over the years ahead.

I was born in good health and was a normal exuberant child until two years old. On Chinese New Year's Day in 1963, my parents returned from work to find me lying on the bed, clearly troubled. Dad sensed something serious and took me to the Calmette hospital. The French doctor told them I had contracted the poliovirus and it had progressed up to my waist. Had they waited another hour in bringing me in, I would not have lived.

I spent most of the next year lying on a bed but many attempts were made to try and get me to walk. My parents did everything to get some life into my legs; rubbing with ginger, exposing me to the morning dew, and sending for a metal-framed contraption from France. Unfortunately nothing made a difference and the family, including me, became resigned to my never walking again.

Mum had another explanation for my affliction. Although an educated professional she interpreted much of the world through a Buddhist lens. She explained my disability as karma, citing the cat whose leg I had accidentally broken. Father, reflecting his Chinese heritage, explained my polio in terms of damage done to bones of a previous ancestor.

However it was to be explained, the polio meant I spent the next two years at the physio-hydrotherapy unit at the Khmero-Soviet Friendship Hospital in Phnom Penh. I could only crawl around as there were no wheelchairs and crutches didn't work for me. If I couldn't crawl I had to be lifted, usually on brothers' or cousins' shoulders.

The extended family that Mum and Dad had allowed to evolve was wonderful for me as I always had someone to help me. I had five older siblings and two cousins on hand to take me where I needed to go. As the decade unfolded, I would have many more half siblings to mentor, boss around, laugh and play with. I was never alone or lonely despite being immobilized.

When I reached the age to go to school at first I wasn't allowed. It was thought by my parents to be too hard – getting to and from school, going to the toilet and generally imposing on my brothers. However I made enough noise to convince my parents that I wasn't going to miss out on school. As a favour to my dad, the owner of the school allowed me to attend when I was six-years-old.

My brothers had to carry me there and back, which they did without complaining. The school was only over the other side of the canal, about 30 metres away! Sadly the teasing that I got about my shuffling around from my peers was too much to bear and ended my first school episode.

As a result my parents got a tutor for me and I learnt to read that way. When I eventually enrolled again in school I jumped a year level because my reading and writing abilities were so well advanced.

Mum's job at the ruling Lon Nol government's censorship bureaucracy meant there were many 'illegal' texts lying around our house, which she had to check for political or religious correctness. She had legitimate access to more literature than most people in the country.

One day, when I came into the area of the house Mum used as a library, I saw many new books with bright colors, written in Khmer script. Among them was a book with pictures and I noticed one in particular of a man with straggly hair who wore long, white robes. He was touching a person who had many wounds all over his body and face. Mum came in and I showed her this picture asking: "Who is he?"

"He is Jesus," she replied

"What is he doing?"

"He is a God of the French, of the Catholics, and he is curing a sick person." I quickly said to my mother to please invite Jesus to come and cure me. But my heart sank when she told me: "He has died already."

'Wouldn't it be nice,' I thought, 'if he could come to my house and cure me so I could stand up and walk like everyone else.' My spiritual path in some ways began at that moment. I felt there was a god and I could expect him to look out for me.

TO HER adopted niece and nephew, Seurn and Prong, Mum was seen as gentle, kind and never harsh. They saw Dad in the same way, appreciating the impact of my parent's kindness on their lives. In contrast Noem, our nanny and wife number two, worshipped Dad but saw Mum as overly strict, and abrasive in disciplining family members.

By the mid 1960's the older children were growing up and starting to make up their own minds about Dad's behaviour. Vanna did not like what she saw, but Wantha viewed it as adult's business. She thought children should respect their parents, and not become involved in their affairs.

Wantha had grown up around boys - *bong* Seurn as well as her younger brothers. She was a strong child, and, perhaps because of the preponderance of males in her life, became closer to Dad than Mum. This was as it had been for Mum who, when her mother had died, became her father's shadow.

Wantha now became her father's personal assistant. At 14 years of age she became his driver, and undoubtedly played a crucial role in allowing him to keep his promises to look after his three families.

Father promised Wantha he would buy her a car when she became a medical student and this helped cement the relationship.

Some days before going to school, Wantha would drop Mum off at work, when Dad wasn't around. She would also take many of the half siblings, Seylo and Noem's children, on walks along the river on Sundays.

Seylo, wife number three, never regarded herself as third in line but wanted to monopolise Dad's affection and time. From where she stood, she was the main wife and her children were as much Bou's responsibility as hers. She continued to work at the Royal Palace and Wantha even drove her to work sometimes and helped run that household.

Some days this situation became too much for both Mum and Vanna, who suffered as the result of Dad's multiple relationships but were powerless to intervene. One day Wantha had brought one of Seylo's children to the doctors and Vanna happened to be already at the surgery.

"Why do you do this for Dad? It is Seylo's family, not yours," she said to Wantha.

"Dad works so hard for all of us, I have to help him. His shirt is always so sweaty because he does everything for us. We should help him as he helps us."

Mum accepted Wantha helping out Dad's other families, but Vanna never did. For Wantha it was a matter of respect to help her father. Dad was upholding his responsibilities to all the families financially and spread his time as equally as he could.

However, Ratana, the oldest son and third child, was a very different story. He had a strong and very special bond with Mum. As Ratana got older he grew to resent Dad and became withdrawn and timid, especially around Dad. In contrast, Mum's concern and affection for Ratana drew him even closer to her, as he realised how his mother really felt about Dad's behaviour. Despite her closeness to her father, Wantha came to believe Ratana had become traumatised by Dad's behaviour and his own inability, as a son, to do anything about it. Just as Wantha became stronger as her father's personal assistant, so Ratana became more withdrawn and dysfunctional as his repellence grew of Dad's treatment of his mother.

By 1968, our home by the canal was overflowing with people and some were ready to move out. By then, Noem had had five children to father, and Seylo had three. (For a complete list of all of Bou's 22 children with four mothers, see Appendix 1) Noem went to live in another house that Father bought for her, as did Seylo.

Vanna was now 18-years-old but had been unable to complete her diploma at school, mainly through being sick and unable to attend. At this point Mum and Dad gave her an ultimatum - either get qualified or get married!

Ultimately the choice was made for her and it was arranged that she would marry a young academic called Sareth. Although initially unwilling to embrace this situation, Vanna came round to the idea.

Once the marriage had taken place, Sareth expected Vanna to quit a job she had just acquired at a bank. However Dad didn't agree with this, giving Vanna a dilemma – to follow her father or her husband. Although she stayed on at the bank, within a year Vanna was expecting her first child.

Bong Seurn was also soon to be married but was still living in the house by the canal. Dara, the girl from Oudong and the first born out of wedlock, was also coming of age and close to being married. Her birth mother had tried to get Dara back a few years before but Dad refused, saying he wanted to look after Dara until her marriage took place.

With three couples in the house all about to start their own families, it could have been expected that they would all go their own way. However this wasn't what Dad wanted. He bought another house, about a kilometre from us, near Kirirom Theatre, and arranged for Vanna and Dara's families to live together in it. Each family had their own room, but shared kitchen and living areas. Part of this was so they could look after each other, but also because Vanna couldn't cook.

In addition to creating this new arrangement Dad gave *bong* Seurn a challenge, as we will see shortly.

Despite having three households to support, Dad agreed with Mum that it was time to rebuild the house by the canal. I remember Rathya and I having to go and live with Noem while this happened. I have warm memories of those months, playing with Rathya and the others. It was undoubtedly a complicated situation for the adults, but I remember only the warmth and affection between us all – especially from Noem, who became like a mother to me.

The new house was a large brick and tile home with wide verandas, two storeys and a rooftop terrace. It was a wonderful new home to move into, with seven bedrooms, mine looking out on to the street below.

There were three large statues of Apsara dancers as you walked up to the second floor. I loved the rooftop terrace as it meant we could have pets there - Ratana raised rabbits. I often sat out there with the other children and we would shout to children on other rooftops nearby.

I had never walked but knew nothing else. Most important to me was being a loved child and sibling in a loving, if broken, family as Ratana called it. However I was blissfully unaware of political and military developments that were about to engulf my country, and then my family.

3

THE CLOCK TICKS DOWN

IN MARCH 1970 our country was consumed by the Vietnam War, or, as it is called in Vietnam, the American War. The peace we had all known as children was about to be snatched away and Cambodia changed forever.

A group of politicians and military leaders, led by the Prime Minister Lon Nol, declared the country to be a republic, so ending the monarchy with Prince Sihanouk as the Head of State. The new government aimed to fight against communism and kick the Vietminh (communist Vietnamese also known as Vietcong) out of Cambodia.

On one side there was the government of Lon Nol and the Americans, on the other the Khmer Rouge (the Cambodian communists) and the Vietcong (and Prince Sihanouk). The middle path that Prince Sihanouk had been trying to chart had disappeared. With three sons approaching military age, the prospect of them being forced to fight in this civil war would soon come to focus my parent's minds.

Ratana was now 14, Chittra 12 and Nora 11 years old. Vanna was married with a son and had moved out while Wantha was 18 and looking at going to university. I was nine and crawled around the house, up and down the stairs, and relied on my brother's shoulders for much else. Younger brother Rathya was my constant companion and we played together a lot with Noem's children.

In 1971, Dad asked *bong* Seurn and his new, pregnant wife to go and look after Dad's old property in Touk Meas. Seurn obliged and was there for around a year before bombs dropped from the sky, either from American or Cambodian airplanes, destroying much of the town.

Such incidents gave people in Touk Meas a stark choice. Stay and risk further bombing and eventually live under the Vietcong/Khmer Rouge, or flee. Seurn chose the latter. He and his wife pushed their bike and carried their children back to Phnom Penh. It took them three days and they had to negotiate roadblocks by both sides of the civil war, as well as the chance of being bombed.

When Seurn arrived back, his family moved in with Vanna and Dara in the house Dad had set up for them near Kirirom Theatre. Seurn had actually gone to Touk Meas as a journalist, but never really liked it much. As you can imagine, under the conditions of a civil war it would have been an almost impossible job.

Seurn and Dara's husband both wanted a job with a salary but did not want to join the army, so decided to join the Military Police instead. One day they both just turned up at home with an army haircut, new uniform and a large 'PM' (*Police Militaire*) on their backs.

Dad didn't really approve, as he didn't want them risking their lives in a pointless war. The logic was hard to fault though, especially as the government became more desperate for soldiers to fight the war.

Seurn felt more at home with this role as a policeman rather than a journalist. Lon Nol's Military Police actually did what police do but, as Dad knew, in the early 1970's Phnom Penh had become a congested, crime-ridden, desperate place for many.

That being said, the two men joining the military police brought an immediate benefit for our family. Chittra got caught up in a demonstration against the Vietnamese near the Independence Monument. He had gone along with lots of other students from his school (Preah Yukunthor High School) but was arrested when things got out of hand. Seurn fortunately found out about it and used his newly acquired influence to get Chittra released and dropped home.

Jails in Cambodia have always been hellholes, and Dad and Mum were very grateful to Seurn once again.

Seurn's sister Prong, a gentle and quiet soul, became the main cook in the house by the canal and would buy food from the market and prepare it for us all. She often had up to 15 mouths to feed so it wasn't an easy job. Mum would return from work mid afternoon and ensure everyone was pulling their weight and being looked after.

Dad often had 24-hour shifts to do and also had to spread his time between his various households - ours, Noem's and Seylo's - as well as having to make occasional trips to the provinces. He would usually arrive home at breakfast time.

I remember sitting round the table one morning, with Mum, Wantha and Rathya. A car door slamming outside told of Dad's arrival and everyone rushed outside to welcome him. I stayed and still remember the bemused and resigned look on Mum's face as everyone left to greet the popular 'guest'.

Following the March 1970 coup, one of the first actions of the new regime was to release prisoners that had been jailed under the old regime. A family friend was one of those prisoners – a former neighbour who had lived two doors down. Our families had spent time together and we had become close. One of his sons used to play his guitar on the rooftop of their house and I would listen admiringly while I fed the rabbits on our terrace. Ratana and I spent a lot of time up there, and the boy next door became something of a childhood fantasy for me.

ALTHOUGH I never met him, President Lon Nol was to have a dramatic impact on my life in a very personal way, thanks to a series of events in the political world that I knew nothing about.

In January 1971 North Vietnamese communist guerrillas snuck into Pochentong airport and blew up our entire air force, as well as killed about 40 of our soldiers. Some time after this Lon Nol had a stroke and left the country to convalesce. When he came back, he brought with him an acupuncturist. Working for the government bureaucracy in an important position, my Mum followed this development and thought that the acupuncturist's skills might help me. It was agreed that I would receive treatment from the acupuncturist, who was a Chinese doctor from France. On most days, *bong* Seurn would carry me over his shoulders into the surgery near the Central Markets.

I was laid on a table and had pins pushed into my legs and waist. They felt like ant bites and were very painful. With over 50 pins being used, I didn't look forward to this daily assault on my body. However, it was said it might give me a chance to walk - which I desperately wanted to do.

Acupuncture is actually very popular in Cambodia, and I stuck to it. After a few days I started to get some feeling back into my legs and this was all the encouragement I needed. Soon I got up from the table and put some weight on my legs. The next stage was being able to take a step or two. Then I was able to walk away from the table, with crutches taking most of the weight. Then I walked with a stick, then finally by myself.

I was ecstatic. I enjoyed every day exploring the world as a walker not a crawler. I could walk to school, Presh Ang Eng Primary School, about 300 metres from home, and not be a burden on my brothers. Dad still wanted them to escort me there but I just wanted to walk with little brother Rathya.

I could now take off to friends' houses when the teachers didn't show up, and be back at school to meet my brothers so my parents were none the wiser. I could shop at the markets and talk to people as an equal, not as someone who appeared so different from them.

When I was 11 years old, I must admit I had resigned myself to a life devoid of much joy and excitement. I already knew that I was as good as anybody else at studying, and languages, if I was allowed to compete. But being able to walk had opened the possibility for me of a full life, with spontaneity and impulse. The doctor had given me hope that this could be mine.

I surged ahead in confidence and soon was even settling a few scores. One day I remember having scored well in a mathematics test. To get a "very good" on the test sheet - I craved that sort of recognition - you had to be one of the first ten to the teacher's desk with a perfect score.

Khuon Vuthy, a boy in my class who gave me a hard time, sat between the teacher and me. As I reached past Vuthy to hand in my sheet, he tripped me and I ended up sprawled on the floor. I was seething inside, but immediately decided there would be no tears. He wasn't going to get that satisfaction.

I waited until recess but never left the classroom. Instead I sat on the floor next to the door and waited for Vuthy to come in. When he did I grabbed his legs, pulled him to the ground and sat on him. Then I punched him in the face as hard as I could until the teacher pulled me off. Revenge was sweet!

In the ensuing investigation Vuthy admitted he had tripped me, and there was just a hint of admiration from teachers and parents alike when they talked about it to me afterwards. The boy never bothered me again.

Ever since that time however I have had an ultra competitive streak in me in test situations. Even as an adult later in life I have to be the first to hand a test in, even if I what have done is not my best. Vuthy's legacy lived on!

AFTER WHAT seemed a whole life of having to crawl around I was now very restless. My parents scolded me for rushing everywhere and being careless. Walking to and from school, I would quite often fall. Also I would climb the stairs to my room too quickly and end up gripping the rail to save myself from plummeting down again.

I just didn't want to stay in one place for long. It was like I had been in a prison before and I wanted to remind myself that I was free.

In 1974 my aim was to skip a year so I could get into the 'petit lycee' (high school) the following year. I doubled up on my study, attempting to do grade eight and seven, one in the morning and the other in the afternoon. This meant enrolling in a private school on Monivong Boulevard - "Debora" - for the grade seven class.

Unfortunately I became unwell that year, and my parents even thought I might have had meningitis, as I had a lot of fever and headaches. They kept an eye on me and we agreed if it got too strenuous I would pull out of the private class.

My cousin Rany, who was sharing my room at the time, was studying English in the evenings that year. I wanted to be part of that as well, but Mum wouldn't allow it and so I stayed in my room and listened to English pop music on the radio. This was actually how I first learnt English and my teachers were the Beatles, the Carpenters, Bee Gees, and Lobo. I would listen to their songs, and then look up the words in my English dictionary.

Despite everything, I kept up with the grade seven and eight programs and passed both. With 1975 looming, I was looking forward to going to the local high school - Tuol Svay Prey.

But the world was changing. The school was three blocks away and soon to become the notorious Tuol Sleng prison run by the Khmer Rouge. These days the school is visited by thousands of tourists each year who see first hand the horror that our lives became.

I attended Tuol Svay Prey for a few weeks in 1975, until the tumultuous events engulfing Cambodia interrupted my life and it became too dangerous to go to school or even outside the house.

My parents knew better than most what was happening with the war on our doorstep. My brother-in-law, Sareth, got to know some Americans and often visited them at the US Embassy. He had been planning to leave for the USA with his young family and knew the Americans weren't going to be able to save Cambodia from the communists.

By 1973 the Khmer Rouge had control over most of the country and it was only a matter of when, not if, they would take over. The Americans stopped the bombing in August, pulled out of South Vietnam and it was obvious they were not coming back to save President Lon Nol or Cambodia from our fate.

From then, my parents started to think about how to get everyone out of the country before the war was lost. Mum focused on her six children. However, Dad by now had 18 dependent children, and at least three women, plus their families, looking to him to sort things out.

Wantha spent most of her waking hours with our father and saw up close what the stress was doing to him. As Wantha said to us: "He sweats for us." Dad knew he would never leave. The families he had created were his life and he would never walk out on that responsibility.

Although not loyal to any individual wife, he loved all his families and his children, and we knew he would do whatever could be done to protect us. Everyone was clamouring for him to get them out and make an uncertain future less scary. But what could he do?

Anyone with any influence and wealth was thinking the same thing. For that reason the government had made it illegal for any military age males to leave the country. It was assumed they were doing this to avoid being conscripted.

Even with money it wasn't easy to leave Cambodia. Assuming you could bribe someone, you had to have somewhere to go and a contact to take you in. Dad had two sisters in France and they were happy, even eager to get his family out. His first family, that is. Their loyalty did not extend to Dad's other families. Dad and Mum had wealth, but a lot of it was locked up in land and jewelry.

Meanwhile normal life was getting harder and harder. The Khmer Rouge had the city surrounded. Travel on roads outside the city became impossible. Supplies had to be brought in by convoy up the Mekong River from Saigon, or flown in by heroic American pilots who risked their lives three times every day, bringing in desperately needed food and fuel. They would land, unload and fly out in a steep spiral to avoid incoming artillery and rocket fire.

Then the Khmer Rouge acquired mines from China, which they placed in the Mekong River, shutting this to our convoys. Close to three million people were now under siege and the noose tightened a little more each day. Thousands starved.

The artillery shells sounded so noisy, even if they weren't close. Rockets had their own noise - a clack-clack sound. At night we wouldn't sleep upstairs and put mattresses on glass doors in case they shattered with vibrations from the shelling. My mirror shook when the shells landed and eventually fell off the wall smashing into pieces.

We only had electricity every second day. Dad allowed our good neighbour, *mak* Sunry, and her family to knock a hole through into our kitchen so her family could crawl through if they felt there was danger from bombs. They used this escape route a lot over the last few months of the siege.

In the first few days of April Dad told us to start filling the car with things in case we needed to leave in an emergency. Despite the shortages, we managed to fill the car with bags of rice, dried food, sugar, salt, oil and cooking pots so that we could leave at a moment's notice. Wantha's VW beetle, her reward from Dad for getting into medical school, held everything. Vanna and Sareth did the same thing, and there was talk of meeting at Aunt Sokhom's house in a village near Phnom Penh, called Prek Eng, if we had to leave the city. Mum and Dad didn't know what was going to happen when the Khmer Rouge marched into town, but they were as ready as they could be.

Wantha could actually have left at any time but refused to leave Dad to manage things on his own. Ratana was given an air ticket out of the country in March 1975, but refused to leave Mum to the machinations of the other wives - as he saw it. Father had managed to secure the ticket for a male child, circumventing regulations, by means of a huge bribe. One million riels changed hands (about $16,000) but it was Chittra who left on that ticket.

Chittra agreed to go to France to live with his aunt and uncle. He flew out on 20 March with a second cousin, as rockets and bombs landed on the airport. When Ratana and Wantha eventually agreed to Dad's entreaties to go, it was too late.

Ratana and Wantha had air tickets to leave for France on 17 April 1975. I also had a ticket to Japan to pursue medical treatment, while Mum was going to leave with Nora and Rathya for Thailand. We all had tickets out, but only Chittra left in time.

Lon Nol flew out of Cambodia in early April, handing over the reins of government to any brave cabinet members willing to remain behind (some did stay). US Embassy staff were helicoptered out on 10 April. The Khmer Rouge moved in from all directions, some of the soldiers seeing the capital for the first time.

On 17 April the government radio, now controlled by the Khmer Rouge announced that the country had a new regime. The revolution was here.

As usual Dad said we couldn't go out and he would be back later in the day after checking up on a few things. He went and visited Seylo, Noem and Vanna to make sure they had everything ready to leave at a moments notice.

We waited all day for Dad to come back. There was still the sound of rockets and artillery, even though the war was supposed to be over. At lunchtime the son-in-law of our neighbour *mak* Sunry came by and told us what he had seen walking from his home.

"There are only Khmer Rouge on the roads. They have tanks, jeeps, and trucks, all full of soldiers waving flags. They have guns and are all dressed in black," he said as we sat in the kitchen. "They had a loudspeaker and said everyone should celebrate the victory. They said peace has come."

"They say the Americans are going to be bombing the city. Did you hear that?" asked Wantha.

"How ridiculous," Mum said as she came into the room. "The Americans have finished with Cambodia now. They won't be back."

"The soldiers are saying we have to leave the city for three days," Sunry's son-in-law continued. "Something about cleaning up the city."

"Where do we go?" I asked.

"To the provinces apparently. I don't know any more than that," he said.

To our great relief, Dad returned around 6.00pm. He had walked a long way having had to leave his car, a Peugeot '404', on the road. He hadn't wanted to draw any attention to himself.

Dad hadn't drunk any water or eaten all day so was very tired but glad to be back with us. He took pride in the day's hardship, saying, with bravado, that he was still a tough soldier.

"They are saying we have to leave the city. Many people have already started to go," he said. "We will have to leave the Peugeot so we will only have Wantha's beetle."

"Dad, is it true it is only for three days?", Wantha asked.

"That's what they say, but who knows. We are ready whatever happens."

"If we keep low and quiet we can just stay here," Mum suggested. "They can't chase everyone out - how would they do that?"

It was quiet that evening in our neighbourhood. The normal sounds of people eating, laughing, arguing or moving around were absent. Everyone was waiting for the morning. Would we really have to leave our house? Maybe the soldiers wouldn't notice us and we could hide here as Mum had suggested. Of everyone in the house that night, only I slept well.

PART 2
MY SECOND LIFE

Survivors from the Khmer Rouge regime, probably around 1980, try and find food and safety.

4

EVACUATION –
A CITY EMPTIES

I WANTED to see what a Khmer Rouge soldier looked like. For years I had to imagine who these people were and now two of them were outside my house. I hobbled over to the window and peered out from behind the curtain of my second story room. Two black-clad men, legs apart, poker-faced were staring at our house. One had a snub-nosed, short rifle and a circle of grenades around his waist. Both wore baggy pants and sandals. The one on the right was young, had a dark face and had clearly been crawling through mud quite recently.

"Open up," the older soldier yelled. He was lighter, taller and wore a peaked hat, with his red and white checked *krama* laced under the strap of a satchel. He ambled the five metres to the house, raised his rifle and banged on the door.

"Open the door and come out, or we will shoot," he said. His partner pulled up his rifle as if to shoot towards the house. Before he had a chance to do that, Dad opened the door.

THE TALL soldier stepped backwards, still facing the house. My father approached him, lowering his head and clasping both hands in a show of respect - called a *sompheas* - a common Cambodian greeting showing humility and respect. It looked odd - the older and wiser elder, genuflecting before these ruffians. They ignored his gesture.

"Good morning comrades. What do you want us to do?" Dad said.

"The Americans are going to bomb the city, so everyone must leave for three days. You must leave now," the older soldier replied.

"Where do we have to go?"

"Go back to your village in the province. We will be back soon to check. You have an hour to leave." The tall one moved closer to dad, eyeballed him menacingly, then left.

As father came back in, all of us had eyes only for him.

"We have to go", he said. "We will stay with Aunty Sokhom at Prek Eng as we arranged, until they let us come back." Then he turned to me and said:

"Laddha, perhaps you can go with *mak* Sunry so you don't have to walk." My panic subsided a little, as I could only walk slowly. I couldn't imagine walking to Prek Eng - it was about 11 kilometres away.

We packed what we might need for 3 days and prepared to leave. I clambered back upstairs, and looked in my bedroom at what I could take. As the teenage daughter of a middle class Phnom Penh family, my world had been full of 'normal' things - books, music, and pet rabbits. I couldn't take any of these things. There was no room. I could only carry my radio.

An hour later we moved off. I was squeezed between cooking pots, rice sacks and boxes in our neighbour's 4-wheeled Lambretta taxi.

People took turns pushing the vehicles as it soon became clear we would run out of fuel quickly with such slow progress. Phnom Penh is a flat city and we easily kept pace with the slow moving crowd of walkers. Behind us, Wantha and my three brothers, carrying what they could, pushing her VW beetle, and Mum and Dad and some other relatives completed our contingent. I knew that somewhere close by, the other wives and their children would be heading out as well. I thought of Vanna and her two little ones.

It took an hour to cover the three blocks to reach Monivong Boulevard, the main southern artery of the city. There we merged into the flood of people heading south. The tide had turned. As war and violence had filled the city with refugees, so now it was emptying.

All around, people were trudging south, watched by the Khmer Rouge soldiers on every corner. Some families were carrying nothing but a child, a sick relative or a basket of food on their head. Others pulled a cart, or pushed a car full of things they weren't going to leave behind.

My skin was glassy with sweat as the sun climbed. It was the worst part of the dry, hot season and an acrid smell of smoke hung in the stifling air. To the north, black clouds drifted up - the last battle of a war that had finally crept up on me.

Until now I had lived the war more worried about the concerns of my parents than any danger to me. Now peace had come, I was feeling the discomfort and stress myself. Peace was meant to make things better. This didn't seem like a good start and it was only the first day.

After about an hour I realized that we had lost touch with my parents. I strained to see past the troubled faces around us, but nobody looked familiar. I felt panicky and nervous realizing that with every minute that passed we were probably drifting further apart. I had never been apart from my family for even a few minutes before and now I was alone.

"We will find them, Laddha, don't worry," *mak* Sunry said, reading my thoughts. She was like family, but at that point I knew that I had no home, no parents and no idea where I would sleep that night. My medication and food were with Mum and Dad. My fever left me too sick to panic so I became numb, withdrawing into myself and shutting out the chaos around me. How could this be happening?

FOUR HOURS later we were nearing the Monivong Bridge, about 5 kilometres from home, when I heard my name.

"Laddha - it **is** you." It was Vanna, my oldest sister. She was outside the Lambretta, walking alongside.

"Oh Vanna. You found me." My emotions surfaced again as I wept and held her tight. "Have you seen Mum and Dad?" Vanna was with her own family and they were also making their way to Prek Eng. It was a complete accident that we had met.

"I don't know where Mum and Dad are, Laddha." Vanna said. "You can just stay with us until we find them. Don't worry!"

I took Vanna's hand and got into the back of a larger truck, the older of my nephews making space for me. Vanna's boys, aged six and two, were there with their father Sareth, and others I knew. Vanna had spotted us as they came close to the familiar Lambretta.

"Thank you for the ride, *om srey*", I called back to *mak* Sunry, not wishing to appear ungrateful for her help. Without it I would have had to walk the whole way. Walking to school was one thing, but this! I cradled my 2 year-old nephew, who was unwell like me, eyes closed, blocking out the day.

"We are going to Prek Eng as well so we will see them there," Vanna said reassuringly. "You are safe now," as she hugged me closely. I smiled at Sareth who gave me the thumbs up. He was pushing the truck with Dara's husband.

How naïve we were. We had no idea of the horror and hardship that would befall us very soon. Worse, we had no idea of the heartache and sadness waiting for us.

When we got to the junction just over the Monivong Bridge we needed to go straight which would take us to the southeast and the road to Saigon and Prek Eng village. But the Khmer Rouge soldiers, the *mit yeung*, would not let us go there.

"Go, go, go!" they insisted, pointing to our right with their guns, towards a place called Koh Krabey. We had no choice but to do what they said. Sareth tried telling them we had to go to Prek Eng but they yelled at him and waved their guns. Sareth raised his hands in the air, and walked away, letting them know he would comply. He didn't want to be another body on the side of the road.

We drove for a while until it looked safe to pull up and think what to do. It was nearly evening by now and many others had the same thought. Families sat down, some prepared food after a long day and others just collapsed where they stopped. One old lady next to us looked like she had nothing left.

Sareth and the others noticed that there were fewer soldiers now so it was decided to try and stay there at least for the night. We parked the truck and set up our camp on the sidewalk, in front of an empty house. The women started to prepare a meal. It became quiet except for the sounds of those suffering from the demands of the day. Coughing and moaning, children crying, broken occasionally by the sharp crack of a rifle shot.

Since turning towards Koh Krabey I had started to notice bodies lying on the side of the road.

"Why are these unconscious people lying on the road," I asked Sareth, as we were eating our meal on the blanket.

"They are dead, Laddha. There is no one to bury them now. Everyone has to leave and some won't make it. Or else they didn't do what the soldiers asked…"

I had never seen a dead body before. They didn't scare me because they looked like they were just sleeping. What did scare me though was knowing their spirits and ghosts were out there in the darkness. I have always been scared of ghosts because they find me and I can see them.

I couldn't fathom how these poor people could just be lying there. Do their family members know they are there? Have they abandoned them without a burial and a ceremony? Have the soldiers chased them away? Could that happen to us?

It was dark and I had never seen some of these parts of Phnom Penh before and certainly not at nighttime. I sought reassurance from Vanna.

"How will we find Mum and Dad? If we can't go to Prek Eng where will we find them?" I asked Vanna.

"Don't worry Laddha. Lots of people know us. We will soon be back home anyway - after this has been sorted out."

Lying awake I tried not to think too much about our predicament. No house, no bed, no parents - instead darkness, dead bodies and ghosts. Other questions drifted in and out of my head. How would we find Mum, Dad and the others? How would we get to Prek Eng? Would we be able to go back to Phnom Penh and live in our house? What would the soldiers do with us next?

5

PREK ENG, FEAR OF THE UNKNOWN

THE NEXT morning, with no shade or shelter, we were woken early by the sun. I was still fevered and trembling. All around us, spilling on to the dusty pavement and into the car-less street, families took stock. Children hovered close to parents, women lit small fires to cook food, and men eyed the soldiers who eyed them back in return.

"What do the soldiers want, Vanna," I asked.

"They are just making sure everyone does what they are told," she said. "It is good to have order. Maybe today we can go to Prek Eng."

Vanna insisted to Sareth that we try to rejoin our parents. The soldiers positioned on the highway would not let us go but they didn't force us to go anywhere else. It seemed like they didn't really know what was going on.

The "three days" came and went and it became clear we were not going back to Phnom Penh any time soon. Our food started to run down and the families with Sareth and Vanna wanted to move on. Tensions grew. I prayed to myself. "If this earth has angels please listen to me now. Let us find Mum and Dad."

Sareth and Vanna thought there must be another way to get to the village apart from along the highway.

"If you head south then swing back to the east you should find a track that leads to Prek Eng," Sareth insisted.

"It's better than waiting around here anyway," agreed Vanna. She stayed with the children but Sareth explored this idea on his bike and soon saw people who knew us. He told them we were trying to find a way to get to Prek Eng and to let Dad know that if they saw him.

After about a week we made contact with him. Someone had told him where we were and he borrowed a bike - from a Khmer Rouge soldier of all people - and eventually found Sareth. They both rode back to where we were and I was delighted when I saw Dad.

We hugged each other tightly but could speak no words. 'The angels had listened,' I thought to myself. 'Thank you, angels.' Father told us that it had taken them three days to get to Sokhom's house. They had pushed the VW all the way there. Noem had arrived but Seylo hadn't turned up yet.

"Good," Vanna said. "Maybe they have gone somewhere else."

"Now, now Vanna. Don't be like that," Dad retorted. "They need us to help look after the children. They will get here soon."

"They can look after themselves. She has her brothers. They don't need us."

"Seylo needs me. She is pregnant and Sakvaney can only just walk. I am their Dad too." Vanna didn't reply but started to pack up ready to move.

It was then I noticed that dad was wearing culottes or short, farmer's pants. He was usually well dressed and clean. A week can be a long time - our comfortable, clean life already seemed like long ago. We all smelled badly, and had few fresh clothes to change into.

We packed up what we could carry on two bicycles, and gave the rest to the other families. They were going to continue south in the truck. We travelled along rough tracks, passing a large pagoda that was full of people camping out. It was slow going, and I walked a lot of it with my stick.

Luckily there was a lot of shade from the many trees that lined the tracks. We stopped often, but had to drink from some dams and ponds, without boiling the water. There were many people in the same situation. The sun was nearly down as we arrived in Prek Eng. We were weary, thirsty, and hungry but I was overjoyed that we were a united family again.

PREK ENG is a village on National Road # 1. This highway skirts the south bank of the Mekong River all the way to Neak Leung, where you can take a ferry across the river and continue east to Saigon. Prek Eng is about 10 kilometres from the Monivong Bridge – it had been a long 10 kilometers.

Unbelievably, Prek Eng still had a functioning market on the main road when we got there. Using medicines, rice, US dollars and riels as currency you could buy a few things, including cakes, chickens, fish, and fruit grown in the surrounding countryside. Prices reflected the extreme situation but, in the minds of some, it was business as usual. A mango that would normally have cost 50 riels, now cost 5,000.

Dirt tracks ran south off the main road leading to rice paddies, plantation fields, fruit trees and houses. To the north, squeezed between the road and the river were simple but established houses. Sokhom's house was in this part, tucked away within a short walking distance to the river. It was a wooden, two-storey building, with the upstairs having one large room and a verandah large enough to hold many of the children who would sleep there over the coming days and weeks. She lived here with her husband, formerly a soldier, and their six children.

The area was reasonably well developed as it was still close to the city but had good soil and access to water from the river. Mangoes, bananas, papayas and pineapples, all grew around here in small plots. You could grow food and still drive to work in the city. Over the coming weeks this environment would provide vegetables and fish from the river, as well as fruit.

Sharing Sokhom's house with us was Noem and her six children. It was crowded and we all slept in or under the house. Because of Dad's forward planning we still had a little rice, and Mum had brought a big bag of cash that was useful as long as the market was open. We would be okay for longer than most. Father and Sareth also went fishing and brought us all some of their catch every day.

Seylo did not arrive until 10 days after the evacuation. When she did, with her parents, brothers, sisters and six children, with one on the way, it drew an ironic laugh from everyone, even Dad. Whereas most people brought rice, clothes and cooking pots, Seylo had brought her TV!

At this time Dad was still stuck in the past. He had built an unlikely and unwieldy family empire, spread out over several houses around the city. Everyone knew their role and played their part, however reluctantly. Now that we were on the move, normal family instincts started to operate for the wives and older children, like Wantha and Vanna. Each family had to look out for themselves, to make their own decisions. But where did that leave Dad? If the families drifted or were forced apart, which family would he choose? For now he was still trying to be all things to all families – and it was tearing him apart.

Perhaps the person who was most aware of our precarious situation was Noem. She had arrived with her six children, the youngest Sopeth, a two- year old boy. She came to Prek Eng, like all of dad's families because he wanted them where he could look after them. Noem worshipped my father so she obliged.

However, she realized that the Khmer Rouge were looking for enemies to kill. If Dad was seen as the patriarch of so many well off and educated families and children, they would label him as an enemy and take him away. She was worried about this and feared for the father of her children.

Mum felt the same way and so the first and second wives started to walk in step. They talked and planned together and felt little in common with Seylo, wife number three. Seylo maintained that she was the best loved of the three wives, which put her at odds with wives one and two.

Seylo did not stay close to us, but in a house a short distance away. Because of this Dad had to choose how he would spread his time and affections across his three families.

Noem's belief in the danger that faced Dad was made more real by the presence of a young Khmer Rouge soldier who would hang around our house, clearly observing, listening and gathering information, even at night time. It was difficult to let the children know what this all meant and to watch what they said. The older ones understood and ensured the little ones didn't talk about things from Phnom Penh.

As a result it was decided that Dad would stay with Seylo only and so prevent the Khmer Rouge from finding out about our complicated domestic situation. This was viewed by Seylo as no more than she deserved. She and her sisters and Dad spent quite a bit of time together. One day Noem and Wantha saw them swimming and having fun in the river as if this was a holiday.

The Khmer Rouge were watching, listening and letting us know what they expected from us. We had to not steal, to hate the "imperialists", to work hard like the peasants, respect women, and more. However we could still move around, didn't have to work, and could talk to who ever we wanted to. I was not well, having a fever I couldn't throw off, so stayed in Sokhom's house.

THEN WE began to notice that people were going missing without explanation. A lady, whose husband Dad knew from work, told him her husband had gone with the soldiers the day before and hadn't come back. Had he seen him? Dad hadn't, but he saw this as ominous.

One day, some soldiers came by and said the new government needed people who could help run services like water and electricity. Administrators and technical people were needed for Phnom Penh, they said. They wanted any such people to come forward and volunteer to return to the city, without their families initially. Father and Sareth talked about this.

Going back to the city would be good, they reasoned, as food was running out here. Maybe the new regime was going to use such educated people after all. However they didn't trust the soldiers. Wantha had been with the adults discussing what to do about this. The children were never included in such discussions and she described the conversation to me later.

"They told us it would be three days and we could go back." Sareth said. "Then they just pretended they had never said that and now we will never be going back. They lied. They have no respect for educated or city people," he continued.

"I don't trust them. They might just want to separate the men from the families. That is more likely. I think we should stay quiet."

Dad and the others agreed they would not volunteer to return. He told them about the work friend who hadn't come back. His wife had been asking the soldiers every day where her husband had gone. They had said they didn't know.

Thousands of men, ready to contribute to a new future, were lured in this way. Most knew of the corruption of the Lon Nol regime and owed it no loyalty. They would have worked for their country given an opportunity, but this was never considered. Finding and killing soldiers and ex-government officials was the immediate priority of the new regime. The adults suspected this but couldn't be sure.

As the days turned into weeks since evacuation, hundreds of thousands of people continued to remain as close to Phnom Penh as they could, hoping to be able to return. The Khmer Rouge wanted us spread all over the country to divide and conquer, and to work in the rice fields as part of their radical plan for the country. They now set about this with renewed vigour, and we would soon be told we had to leave.

6

THE SCATTERING OF
THE FAMILIES

BONG SEURN had also arrived at Prek Eng with his wife and three children as well as his father, Try, and other relatives. Having been a Military Policeman for the Lon Nol regime, Seurn knew that he was in great danger if the soldiers found this out. He thought it likely they would, and did not want to place his family in harms way by their association with him.

He very quickly decided he would leave for Touk Meas on his own, making the heartbreaking decision to rely on relatives to look after his wife and children. He came to me to say goodbye. *Bong* Seurn would always have a special place in my heart for lifting me each day on his shoulders for months to get my acupuncture treatment. We hugged and wished each other luck. The next morning he was gone.

Noem then stated that both she and Seylo should release my father from his responsibilities to their families and leave the village. This was a generous and brave position to take as it meant she would have to live without the support of Dad and the rest of the family she had known ever since she had come to live with us. Seylo however was having none of it.

"My children are younger than SutChay's," she insisted, backed up by her sister who was with her. "Everyone else should leave so my children will have their father. I will give birth soon. I need Bou here with me." Noem could have made a similar claim, but didn't. That just wasn't her style.

It was a heartbreaking discussion. There was so much at stake. No one knew what was going to happen. In normal circumstances staying together would be our strength. But this was far from normal and it seemed unwise to stay together with Dad becoming known as the head of three families.

Wantha, now aged 23, and Mum made the decisions for my family and they were afraid for all of the children who they loved like their own, no matter who the mother. How could you choose who to try and protect? There were seven children under ten years old between Noem and Seylo's families.

Seylo's attitude seemed selfish, while Noem, my second mum, worried so much about Dad, rather than herself. When Noem said shortly after that she was going to Kampong Cham, mother tried to talk her out of it.

"We should stay together Noem. If you can't then at least leave Sopheavy with us to take care of her," she said to Noem. The seven-year-old was my mother's favourite and she wanted to keep her to ensure she was okay. Noem would not consider such a thing.

The soldiers said to Noem's children that if they wanted to eat rice they should go on the boat. Her children were hungry and said to their mum they wanted to go on the boat. By next morning she, and her six children, ranging from Nareth, aged 15, to Sopheth, her two-year-old boy, were gone. She didn't tell anyone – not even Dad.

When he found out that one of his wives had acted without consulting him, he was incredulous. Dad believed only he could protect them but couldn't see that each of the wives had to make their own decisions in this pressure-cooker situation.

He found out that they had left on a boat, and went to the river to investigate. For some reason, he thought he could still find her, and wanted all of us to follow him to bring Noem and her children back. Seylo and Mum refused what was clearly an unreasonable proposition. He was getting desperate and wanted to go on his own to try and find his lost family but Seylo convinced him to stay.

A week later the soldiers told us we had to leave. There was a chance at that time that we could have taken a boat to Vietnam. Dad saw someone he knew on a boat and the offer was there. He would have accepted but for Noem not being there. His family, he said, was 'incomplete'.

He decided that his remaining families would stay together and head for a village called Kraingyew, in Koh Thom district, about 60 kilometres south of Phnom Penh. This was the plan and Seylo and Mum agreed. Vanna, with her two young boys, and her husband Sareth, were going to stay with us as well.

WE SET off from Prek Eng several weeks after arriving there. We pretended to be two separate families but stayed within range of each other. We trudged slowly away, setting a pace dictated by having many young children who had to walk. I walked slowly with a stick, trying to conserve what little energy I had. We rested after lunch if it was hot, and tried to find some shelter by night. We were now well into the rainy season, and had no means of keeping dry. We slept under the stars and the moon, and now thought wistfully about Prek Eng where we at least had a roof over our heads.

Dad's plan to keep in touch with us and Seylo's family lasted for a few days. Mother's heart however was not in it. She felt we were on this trek to nowhere just to please Dad. Food was already running low with so many mouths to feed in our group. There was nothing waiting for her there. She was morose and uncommunicative. When the Khmer Rouge soldiers said they wanted to send people to their homeland, she saw an opportunity to go back to the land of her childhood – Battambang.

She had grown up there with her father, Naow Pan, and had many relatives scattered around that province. But if she were to go there with us, Dad would have to choose which family to be with. This made it more difficult to broach with Dad.

Wantha, Vanna and Mum talked to each other and then with Dad, making the case for going to Battambang and splitting the families. He was against this of course as he was not one to delegate to others the responsibility for looking after his family. But he gradually came round to the idea, swayed by the knowledge that Vanna, and her husband Sareth, would take care of Mum, and our family.

And so it was agreed. Dad would continue on with Seylo to her homeland. Family number one, with Vanna and her family, would wait for the bus to Battambang, which the soldiers said was being arranged. Returning to Prek Eng was not allowed. Dad expected to come and find us once he had settled Seylo into her new home.

THE PLAN started unraveling almost straight away. Our family was told to wait by the road for a bus to Battambang. But when they saw that Vanna had her own family, they said she could not come with us.

Mum argued with the soldiers.

"We are a family. This is my daughter. These are my grand-children," she pleaded to the young, grim-faced soldiers, grabbing Kaddheka "They have to come with us. They need us."

"They cannot go with you. They are another family." The soldier was very young and had no concept of compassion, negotiation or being reasonable. He had his orders and the power over us to enforce his will.

"NO! NO! If they can't come with us we will stay here with them," Mum said, losing any fear. "We won't go to Battambang,"

"We want to stay together," Vanna echoed Mum.

"Only *Angka* decides where you go and what you do! *Angka* will look after you now. Then he lifted his gun to ensure there was no doubt as to who was in charge. We had no idea who or what this "*Angka*" was, but didn't want to ask.

"(*Khbaal ana, saak anung*" (translates to 'whose head, their hair') he said, in one of those statements that the Khmer Rouge had invented to sum up their ideology. It meant that family was no longer important – now *Angka* would play this role. Your loyalty must now be to *Angka*. It was part of the plan to divide families so people were isolated and easier to control.

For Vanna it meant leaving her mother and younger siblings

and forsaking them to an unknown future - to the whims of these unfeeling, angry black-shirted 'winners' of our war.

For mother, she was being forced to part from her first-born child and her only grandchildren. She would also have felt even more vulnerable now that Dad had gone and Vanna would soon be gone. For Wantha, she was losing her best friend of twenty years. Her heart was breaking. For the rest of us, we had no way of making sense of this. The more I thought about it the more helpless I felt.

The bus did not come that day and Vanna and Sareth moved a little away from us but close enough to come back and see us until they were moved on. The next day she came back with her two sons, the 6-year-old Kaddeka and 2-year-old Karuna. They loved being with their cousins and grandma, but were hungry and sick.

How sad a time that was. We knew we would soon be parted, maybe forever, and had some time to hug and talk and play. But the talk was full of fear and pain and not knowing, of lives slipping out of control. We were at the mercy of the soldiers, who seemed to come from another universe. And here we were standing by the side of the road, starving, sick, and powerless to change any part of our situation.

The next day no bus arrived and again the next day. For ten days we stood and waited under the sun, in the rain and beneath the stars. Vanna came each day but we never said goodbye. Wantha assured her that she would take over the role of looking after Mum. When the bus did come, we knew we would not see Vanna and our two nephews again. We were relieved to know we were on our way but desperately sad for our parting.

OUR FAMILY now comprised Mum, Wantha, myself, my three brothers plus Prong, our female cousin. The bus arrived and we all boarded but had to wait, as the bus didn't move for a while. They were still waiting for some more families.

Then I looked back behind the bus and there he was – Dad!

He was about 15 metres away, with Seylo's brother.

"Dad, Dad," I called out to him through the window. When he

got near the bus he climbed up and asked us if we were going to Battambang now. He looked around and saw that Vanna was missing. We told him what had happened. Mum did not say a word, but tears rolled down her cheeks.

Dad now had to consider what difference this made to his rapidly evolving plans. Vanna and Sareth had been going to look after us, but that wasn't going to happen now.

He hugged us one by one. Ratana, at 19 my oldest brother, looked his usual disapproving self. Nora, 17, was crying as loud as I was. My younger brother Rathya, 12 years old, when he saw us crying, started sucking his thumb and weeping. Dad then hugged me tightly and I would not let him go. People on the bus thought we were a strange family, as they did not know he was our father.

Dad then said to Wantha, the oldest sibling,

"Take care of your brothers and sisters and little Laddha."

"I am very proud father, I will remember your words," Wantha said with tears streaming down her face now as well. "I want to show my feelings. I have a father but I cannot call him 'Dad'."

With Wantha's last words Dad looked at her. He was speechless but mumbling. No words could sum up his dilemma. Either he stayed with Seylo's family and ignored the fact his first family had no guardian. Or he went with them and left Seylo's young family to their own devices.

He couldn't live with either choice. He would be abandoning a family whichever way he chose. Dad had always been there for all his children and his wives. It was unthinkable that he could desert his own blood.

He looked down momentarily then suddenly turned and got off the bus. He went straight to Seylo's brother, who was waiting with the bike.

"Tell your sister I am going to Battambang with SutChay," he said. "Take these clothes and give them to Seylo. I will come back when I can." And then he handed over some clothes and climbed back on the bus. He only had the clothes he was standing in. He sat down next to me and embraced me, his tears and mine mingling as we cuddled. I was so happy. He chose us. He chose Mother. He chose me.

He always said that among his 24 children I was the one who redeemed all their sins for them. I played this special role on behalf of the others. I never really knew what to make of that, except that Dad loved me and thought me 'special'.

As we pulled away from the side of the road the heavens opened up and the rain fell so hard it was like someone was angry. I had thought it unlikely Dad would ever live with us again but he was still here. We didn't have Vanna but we had Dad. God had given my family a reprieve - for now.

7

PREY VENG PONG TEK

BEFORE 1975, Father had no enemies that I knew of. He loved to cook French food, but was not home much. He worked hard as a Customs Officer, as he had to in order to take good care of his ever-growing family. He never smoked or drank, unlike Mother who smoked a little and enjoyed a wine or two at meals. He hated corruption and his Customs 'team', was often recognized by winning awards.

On the bus, my Dad sat silently with the rest of us as the driver of the bus turned left instead of right when he reached the National Road # 5. To go to Battambang was north and we should have turned right. Nobody knew what this meant. However we were not waiting long for an answer as the bus stopped at a pagoda called Prey Veng Pong Tek, near the Prey Sar prison called T3. This village was much smaller than Prek Eng and required an ox-cart to get around.

We were met by a group of Khmer Rouge soldiers who were very harsh, ordering us to get off the bus and take our things. This was the first time I felt the intensity of their hatred. They were so young and dismissive of us. We were now a smaller group than we had been at Prek Eng. The relative calm and freedom we felt there was gone. Now we felt the glare, the intolerance - the gulf that separated us from them. Things had definitely changed. We knew we were in real danger.

We didn't even ask why we were not going to Battambang. We got into a line and waited to be told what to do next. Our group was told to stay in the Pagoda.

We started living inside the decaying complex, constantly in fear of the soldiers. Staying in the pagoda itself suggested that we were not going to be here for long, and so we were afraid of what might lay in store for us.

One night Mum took me outside of the pagoda to urinate. Given my disability and fear of the dark she would usually make that journey with me. While I was sitting in the darkness I thought I saw a large ghost and screamed loudly! I have always been afraid of ghosts. The 'ghost' got a fright from my screaming and jerked upwards, banging his head on a wooden beam. The whole building seemed to shake.

The ghost was actually a Khmer Rouge soldier and he thought I was a threat to him because it was so dark. He yelled out in anger and pointed his gun at me, demanding to know why I had screamed at him. I was paralysed with fear. I couldn't speak and Mum also couldn't find any words to calm his irrational terror.

Dad appeared however and managed to talk quietly to the soldier and convinced him I was a scared child and of no danger to him. Finally the soldier walked away. Dad saved me. That night I could have died by being shot if not for him. Was this just good luck? I don't think so. That night I felt God had protected me again.

We were now scared to talk openly when the soldiers were within earshot and Dad told us that we had to hide our past from them. One day soon after we arrived, friends of my father from Phnom Penh (one was the owner of the Samamki Hotel) came past in front of where we stayed. He, together with another city dweller and two Khmer Rouge soldiers, asked my father to come with them as they said they had to find some wood to make coffins in a nearby village. My father said

"I am not yet finished cutting the firewood as you can see."

"But if we have many people," his friend replied, "we can finish this work early and come back home together." Father hesitated to join them but one of the soldiers came over and told him he had to come.

"There is a lot of the day left, we have to do this now." His words suggested a reasonable, logical plan, but the angry tone of his voice and attitude, left no doubt it was about something else. Dad had no choice. Reluctantly he went with the group as they ambled out of the pagoda and round the corner out of sight. I watched them leave. I remember Dad had his *krama* round his neck. Just like that, he was gone.

He didn't come back that night, and another day passed. Mother and Wantha all asked the soldiers where my father was. I remembered the lady in Prek Eng who had asked the same people the same questions. They said he would be back soon when he and the others had finished making all the coffins. They had to find wood in the forest they said.

MY MOTHER waited three days and then went to the temple in the pagoda to pray to the Buddha. She promised to sacrifice her hair for my father if he could come back safely. A week passed and, despite mother shaving her hair, my father did not return from making the coffins.

I was naive and was reassured by Wantha, Mum and Ratana that Dad was okay.

"Maybe he went to Kampong Cham to find Noem and look after her children," they said. He had talked about this a lot and lost sleep over it. "Maybe he escaped from this bad place? Maybe he would be back tomorrow? Maybe he went back to Seylo?"

Mum and Wantha always prayed to the Buddha statues in the pagoda for Dad. They continued to ask the soldiers what had happened to him, but got no answer. As the days went by I slowly came to accept the rumours. It was whispered that the soldiers had killed all of the men who went with them that day.

Deep down I knew my dad was no longer alive. My wonderful, incorrigible father. The man who loved three wives and 24 children was gone forever. The father who chose me – was dead.

Now we started to mourn Seng Bou - father and husband. Mum was reduced to saying nothing and we all cried noiselessly. The tears trickled down sad faces. How terrible a time in that place! We were from a comfortable and respected family in our old life, but now we were like beggars and paupers and prisoners in a 'prison without walls'.

From what I know now of the ways of the Khmer Rouge, I imagine my dad died soon after being taken away. He had been identified as part of the old regime and so it would be assumed he was an enemy of what came to be called *Angka* - the 'organisation'.

In the first few weeks of the new regime many thousands of those identified, or just suspected, of potential disloyalty were executed. They were taken far enough from the village so nobody would know what happened. It was never revealed what had become of missing loved ones. It just wasn't talked about.

8

CHA HUOY, HELL ON EARTH

NOW WE were on our own, without the protection of my father. After one month at Prey Veng Pong Tek, the Khmer Rouge soldiers decided to move us to another place. No one dared ask them where we were going but I was glad to be moving. This place had taken our father and I was in constant fear of what may happen next. One morning we boarded one of many buses that began moving people to the northwest. At last, it seemed, we were going to Battambang.

We were all hungry, sick and the driver drove too fast, scaring me a bit more. We had a little cooked rice but I gave mine to Rathya, as he seemed to need it more than me. Some time in the afternoon we pulled up on the side of the National Road # 5 and saw many ox-carts lining the road on both sides. Thousands of people were being dropped off here, next to the Svay Daunkeo pagoda, on the border between Pursat and Battambang provinces. We were about two thirds of the way from Phnom Penh to the city of Battambang.

Battambang is in the north west of Cambodia and runs from the shores of the Tonle Sap Lake, a huge water body that grows and shrinks with the seasons, westwards to the jungle-clad mountains that border Thailand. National Road # 5 cuts through the middle and is the main road between Phnom Penh and Thailand.

We were told by the soldiers there was food being given to everyone and so there was - one *spoonful* of uncooked rice for the whole family! How could we feed a family with so little?

For some reason we were then given a choice about which village we would go to. There were three to choose from, and we knew nothing more than the name about each. We had chosen Cha Huoy because it means jelly in Khmer, which made it sound friendly. We soon discovered this was in the direction of the mountains, and so we headed into the night along a track away from the main road.

We lived in a constant state of flux and our experience told us we should not believe anything the soldiers told us. Uncertainty was the only thing we could rely on.

We had arrived late at night in a village that had no knowledge of our coming and had made no preparations for us. Cha Huoy is about four kilometres off the main road. The whole group, over 4,000 families of New People (*neak thmey*), trudged to a windswept, treeless open stretch of rice fields. We dropped to the ground as soon as we could. My family huddled together on mats to keep off the cold night, trying to make our single blanket cover us all. Although we had mosquito nets we had nothing to tie them to, so they were useless. We slept the best we could until the sky started to lighten in the east and we woke to our new 'home'.

Since leaving Prey Veng Pong Tek, we had all become more sick, hungry and dehydrated. Our group now comprised myself, my mother, older sister Wantha, my three brothers - Ratana, 19, Nora, 15, Rathya, 12, - and our female cousin Prong. The three boys and I had dysentery, which is like a bloody diarrhea. We lay on our mats, unable to move far or help the rest of the group with securing the necessities of life.

Wantha and Prong were the least unwell so went off to try and find water to wash ourselves, drink and cook with. They could not find any clean water and no one from the local village made any effort to help us. Eventually Wantha and Prong found some dirty water that we boiled and used to drink. There was also no food so the girls wandered further away to gather anything they could that we could eat to ease the gnawing hunger in our bellies. They returned later in the afternoon with insects, leaves and a lizard. The other families around us fared no better and shared our distress.

The next night was the same and the one after that. Once again we were out in the open, with no roof over our heads. We could avoid neither the heat of the day, the cold of the night or the rain, which seeped into everything. Mother tried to find out when we would be given some shelter, some relief from this muddy, putrid squalor. We were given no reassurance that it would end any time soon. On the contrary we were made to feel ungrateful, that we were complaining unnecessarily, and that we were weak. Days turned into weeks. Wantha and Prong continued to forage, going further and further away, sapping the little energy they had.

This was surely hell on earth. All of us, thousands of city dwellers, had been used to buying our food in markets and having regular meals in our houses, which had toilets and medical facilities nearby. The Khmer Rouge had removed all of those things from us but put nothing in their place. As there was no sanitation and many people had dysentery and diarrhea, the field became smellier and smellier. As I lay with my brothers I just wanted water to drink and wash myself with. There was nowhere to get away from any of this. Mother tried to console us but could only offer words and was herself unwell.

We were given very little food each day – the standard one spoonful of uncooked rice for every family. No meat, no other food, no salt, no sugar. Luckily we kept some salt hidden in a water bottle and used it to give some taste to whatever we could find to eat. Wantha decided to try and trade a precious Citizen watch she had received from our parents for passing her first year medicine exams. Unfortunately she wasn't good at trading and she only got one *prahok* (fish) and some uncooked rice for it. Ten *prahok* would be needed to make a meal for us all.

One day we found some banana trees, chopped them and boiled the trunks. I felt like an animal, foraging for leaves, scraps, and insects - anything to relieve the hunger that haunted us.

There were other stresses for us city dwellers. One night soon after we arrived we were woken by a shriek from Wantha. "Aieeeee!" she cried, jumping up and throwing something off her. It was a snake, about a metre long. We were lucky it hadn't bitten us. By the time

I realized what was happening it was gone and the danger passed. However I was still trembling with fear from being woken from a deep sleep by such a scream and didn't sleep any more that night. In Cambodia a snake is a portent of something bad going to happen and my mother saw it this way too.

With so little food and no medicine it was only a matter of time before either illness or starvation picked off those most vulnerable. Ratana, the oldest boy, was the most sick of us all with dysentery and had hardly moved from his mat since we arrived. With dysentery you have diarrhea with blood in it and lose whatever nutrition you may have consumed before the body can absorb it. Ratana lacked energy and, with no medicine and little food, could do nothing to halt his slide. Mother's favourite child was dying before her eyes and there was nothing she could do.

Within a week of coming to Cha Huoy, Ratana passed away. The son who had taken her side, who had believed vehemently in her place as the only matriarch – he had chosen her and now he was gone. Not only that but Wantha had lost her playmate and childhood confidant.

After Ratana, we wondered who would be next. Nora and I were unwell, and mother was fading away from starvation. Rathya, at 12, the baby of the family, appeared the healthiest of us all. He managed to stay clear of malaria and fevers and, with Wantha, seemed the most likely to survive.

In Khmer culture and history there is a legendary hero called Khleang Meung. Centuries ago, in a time when the Khmers were fighting our perennial enemies the Thais, a stalemate developed between the two armies. In order to gain a decisive advantage, Khleang Meung chose suicide so he could call upon the Army of Ghosts to help beat the Thais. He threw himself on poisoned spikes, killing himself but summoning the Ghosts and winning the battle.

A rumour had started among the desperate and starving population in the Cha Huoy region that the spirit of Khleang Meung was coming to take hundreds of 12-14 year olds away, so they would live with him. Mother knew of this, though Ratyha did not. Mother prayed to the spirit of Khleang Meung not to take Rathya and, to that end, tried to find a bird to set free as an offering. In Khmer culture releasing birds is a way to redeem sin, making it less likely bad things would happen.

Mother traded some *len* (silk) she had for two birds from the local villagers. She and Wantha released the birds and prayed that Rathya would not be taken. Rathya was just two years younger than me and we got on so well and were very close. We played together a lot and I was always there for him as he grew up. In return he looked out for his crippled big sister at school.

Shortly after, Rathya started acting strangely, as if he had a spirit inside him. He told us he had seen a man in a dream with a strip of red cloth on his arms and neck, and that this man wanted to take him away with him. Mother thought that this vision was Khleang Meung. Later that night Rathya went to sleep and never woke up. Mother could not believe it and cried so much, as did all of us. She had lost another son. Even Khleang Meung it seemed was capable of betrayal.

After three weeks of sleeping in an open field, so many people had died that there was space for us in huts that were being built in Cha Huoy by the *neak moulthan* (the original villagers). The huts were in straight rows and made of bamboo and thatch, raised off the ground about a metre to keep above the sometimes-flooded ground. Each hut, about three metres by four metres was divided into four parts, with a family given one corner each.

As we moved our mats we found termites had moved in underneath and had actually eaten away parts of them. I remember thinking it was lucky that they hadn't managed to crawl into our ears while we slept as how would we ever have gotten them out?

Nora, now 15, was the naughty boy of our family. He was the middle son and middle child and often incurred Father's wrath. When he was naughty, father would call out sharply "*kon aeng!*" (which roughly translates as 'child, manage yourself'). Nora always had friends around and was smart, excelling at school.

Soon after arriving at Cha Huoy, Nora had developed diarrhea. Access to clean water was a critical issue at the time. Other ailments also added to Nora's poor condition, and, just after we moved into the huts in Cha Huoy, he was taken to the medical centre in the village. There was no medicine there or trained medical staff however, and soon someone brought us the news that he had died, alone.

Wantha and Prong went to the hospital and took his body and buried him in a field somewhere close by. Mother sat expressionless. She did not move, nor did any tears roll from her eyes. Of her three sons who remained in Cambodia all were now lost.

Mum had lost three children in only a month. No mother should have to suffer this. She was so sad and became lifeless and devoid of any emotion. She had a gastric illness and, even though we now had shelter from the rain and sun, she could no longer talk or hold any food or water down. She could only make noises like "la ... puuuuu ... "and point to her throat. Mother lost so much weight her bones stuck out and she looked like a seven-year-old. She did not cry at all. Wantha tried to find rice and medicine for her but there was none anywhere.

I remembered when I was young and mother would wake up early in the morning before going to work, and carry me in her arms to the garden to massage my legs with the dew from the grass. Other days she would boil ginger and try and get some stimulation in my legs, although nothing she could do made any difference. Our darling mother, our rock, our proud and strong Pan SutChay, was wasting away before us. I could do nothing to repay that love, nothing to give back to her now she needed me.

On the evening of 6 January 1976, mother went to sleep between Wantha and I. We woke at midnight to find she had passed away. We don't know when. Wantha and I cried and hugged each other. She told me to stay with Mother while she went and told Prong who was at a nearby camp.

It was only me with mum's corpse, together for the rest of that long, dark night. I was scared because of thoughts about ghosts and it felt like a very long time before Prong and Wantha came back. We all cried and cried together before finding some white cloth and material to cover Mother's body. In the morning they took her body away from the village to bury her. I couldn't help them as I couldn't walk and was too unwell with diarrhea. Because of this I don't know where my mother is buried and cannot go to her grave. My heart still hurts so much because there is no grave for my mother or my father or my brothers.

9

A 'BRAVE NEW WORLD'

IN THE new, utopian world that began on 17 April 1975, there were essentially three classifications of Cambodians.

Firstly, there were 'Old People' or *neak moulthan* as they were known in Cha Huoy - the people for whom the revolution had been made. They were the uncomplaining, hard working, villagers who toiled daily to grow rice to feed the nation. Together with the Khmer Rouge soldiers and officials (and behind them *Angka*, literally meaning 'organisation') the *neak moulthan* now had the power to run the country.

There was a second group called *neak 17*, (named after 17 April 1975 when Khmer Rouge forces entered Phnom Penh) which comprised country people who had been forced to flee their home because of the civil war. They were regarded by the new rulers as redeemable if they worked hard and did what they were told.

The last group, the New People or *'neak thmey'*, were the city dwellers who were viewed by the rulers as lacking the moral fibre engendered by a life of toil in the rice fields. They were the enemy who would forever find a way to resist the revolution. Unlike in other revolutions, such as in Vietnam, however, the non-believers would not be given a chance to be re-educated but simply left to die or be killed. All that had to be done was to identify them.

Framing things in this way made New People continually vulnerable to allegations of undermining the revolution by their actions or ideas. A broken tool, an injured foot, a verbal challenge – all could be construed as betrayal and hostility to the revolution. It also allowed the new rulers to treat the New People as sub-human and look away while they starved to death.

In the first year in Cha Huoy most of the New People died this way. Of course this group contained almost all the doctors, nurses, teachers, engineers, and administrators available to the country. These people had been educated and lived in the city, and to the Khmer Rouge soldiers - in the main, uneducated, violent, hate-filled teenagers from the countryside - the loss of these people and their skills was irrelevant.

For those few New People who were left alive, they had to continually earn the right to be part of the new society. There was only one way to do that - by planting, growing and harvesting rice and following orders without question or complaint.

My father had been killed in the 'first wave' of repression. Subsequent waves would target new groups within Cambodian society but New People were always mistrusted, and regarded as disposable. As the new regime said, "to keep you is no gain, to kill you is no loss."

At the village level, the mobile work teams, or *chalats*, were given the best workers. Everyone else was initially kept at the local village, either to look after the children, or to work in or around the fields near the village. The *neak moulthan* in the villages now decided who would do what, how much food everyone would get, and all the other decisions that mattered.

The *mit yeung*, the Khmer Rouge soldiers, were always around to enforce the whole system. They would execute, punish, torture as they wished and were only answerable to *Angka* - a distant and vague authority that cared only about rice production and staying in power.

I HAD serious diarrhea and a regular fever, as well as hemeralopia or night blindness. The latter was caused by a lack of vitamins and around evening it became hard for me to see clearly. It was expected that I would die because of my poor health and sickly nature.

While I was still alive, I felt vulnerable knowing that at any time I could succumb like my brothers or like the disabled people that I had previously seen around the village. There had been other polio sufferers at Cha Huoy when we arrived, but they weren't around any more.

I now relied on Wantha to help keep me alive - to ensure I got to the meals, to do the little things that could make the difference between life and death at this time.

Wantha and Prong were told they would both be in a female *chalat* whose leader was a 40 year old woman called *mit* Pet. Wantha pleaded with her for both of them to be allowed to remain and look after me. *Mit* Pet was unmoved and said only one of Prong and Wantha could stay with me. Prong, my gentle, loving cousin, who had cooked for us all in our house by the canal, said she would go and Wantha could stay.

Prong knew it meant hard work, little food and sleeping out on the fields. The workers in the *chalats* never knew where they were going and rarely left the fields they were working in if they were a long way from the village. They ate where they worked, the watery rice gruel being brought out to them. If it rained, the drops would splash from the filthy ground into their bowl, diluting and polluting an already watery soup. At night the 'slaves' could work until well after dark and just lay down where they were, to sleep for a few hours. If it rained, their skin never got a chance to dry.

Soon after leaving us, Prong came back sick and Wantha had to go to the *chalat* in her place. Prong did not get better but went to the medical centre where she passed away, alone. Seurn's sister, our cousin and another spirit from our house by the canal was gone.

IT WAS now just Wantha and I. We only had each other. Wantha had remained relatively free of illness and, despite having lost most of her family, knew what she had to do to survive - work hard and never complain about anything. However her assertive temperament was always going to be a risk in triggering a violent reaction from the *neak moulthan*.

Shortly after my mother's death, the *mit yeung* decided they were going to roll out another part of the new society and arrange marriages for any of the New People they decided were suitable. No one had any choice about a partner, but were just told they would be taking part. As Wantha was apparently a healthy, single female in her mid-twenties she was told she would be getting married – and she refused.

Perhaps Wantha had seen first hand how Cambodian men could treat the women in their lives and had decided she could never allow herself to be part of such an arrangement. She was much too strong and independent a character to play second-string to anyone in a marriage.

"I am already married comrade," she told the *neak moulthan*. "I have just lost touch with my husband. He may be here soon. What will happen when I meet him if I marry again?"

This was of course a lie but for many young people in a similar situation it was true. The *neak moulthan* weren't interested in anything she had to say. As Wantha continued to resist, the threats increased. Initially she was told she would marry a *neak 17*, but then warned that if she would not comply with this she would have to marry a disabled *mit yeung*.

The *neak moulthan* knew I was her sister and maybe thought this would move Wantha. It didn't. She still wouldn't agree. Looking back now, both of our lives could easily have ended at this time. Two things however conspired to save us.

Firstly *mit* Pet. She was one of the *neak moulthan* simply because she had lived in this village her whole life. She had no education, was illiterate and married with two children. Despite having lived in the countryside, no one in her family knew much about farming, not even her husband. He had fallen in with the *mit yeung* for much the same reason as his wife and could now 'lord' it over the New People.

Wantha was assigned to Pet's *chalat*. At first *mit* Pet behaved towards Wantha in the typical *neak moulthan* way, driven by hatred and jealousy. Pet was a harsh ruler and forced Wantha to dig channels between the rice paddies even when she was aching and trembling from malaria. She ridiculed Wantha saying she had "rabbit fever", meaning it was a pretense. She jeered that her body shook like a tractor yet she still ate rice so well.

Despite the extreme lack of food and medical attention, and deaths of so many people, it was assumed by the *neak moulthan* that saying you were ill or felt weak was likely a ploy to get out of work.

However after some time Pet became swayed by Wantha because she always worked hard and did not complain or pretend she was ill. Wantha was also an outgoing, friendly, female and Pet began to pity, then respect her rather than detest her.

Over the next two years a kind of 'dance' developed between the two. *Mit* Pet would occasionally give Wantha extra food - some pumpkin, other times more rice. This happened only a few times but made the difference between Wantha's surviving or not.

This unusual relationship seemed to have run its course however when Pet called Wantha to see her late one night. Exhausted after a long day Wantha went to Pet's hut.

"Wantha I have bad news," *mit* Pet said softly, struggling to raise her voice or find her words. "At the meeting today they say you are an enemy of *Angka*." Wantha looked down not knowing what to say. To be an 'enemy of *Angka*' was to be dead.

"I do everything you ask and work hard for *Angka*," Wantha said after a moment. "Do they not see that?"

"They say you have light skin like a Vietnamese and that you can read and write." Then the emotions building up burst and Pet cried.

"I told them you are good for *Angka*, that you work, but they won't listen," she sobbed. "They said 'is she your favourite'? I said she is not Vietnamese. She can read but many people can. I know her and she works hard without complaining." Wantha was quiet. A few moments later, Pet said.

"You are like my daughter. I don't want to lose you ... but they wouldn't listen. They know you won't marry so they find this excuse."

Wantha knew her life was slipping away, and knew that Pet was her only hope, as a mother would be to her daughter. In that moment, of confronting her mortality, Wantha felt like a daughter to Pet. A bond was forged. Something had changed that couldn't be taken away. But it looked like it was too late.

Wantha left the hut knowing she had been sentenced to death. How she survived involved a Khmer Rouge soldier called mit Tang. I will leave this part of the story until later, as it has a bearing on other things.

A FEW months into 1977 Wantha left in a *chalat* and we lost track of each other. We had no idea if the other was alive or how she was doing. As the days became weeks I realized I was now well and truly on my own. No parents, no big brothers or sisters. Whatever happened from here was up to me.

10

ALONE

I NOW lived alone and used a stick for walking. Like everyone else, I was very weak because all we were fed was a watery, rice gruel with no meat or vegetables. With no vitamins or variety of nutrition our bodies shriveled and many New People died.

The region has a bad mosquito problem and I caught malaria. With no medication I was constantly laid low with fever, aches and chills. Despite everything, I was still expected to work hard and not complain.

When we first came to the village there was a lot of noise. Every morning the children would sing a song of *Angka* as they headed to work in the fields. There had been four families living in each of the huts built for us after we moved in from the fields.

Now there was no noise. Almost everyone had either died or been moved to a new work camp.

Even with my lack of mobility and difficulty doing anything physical I was still ordered to work with the other New People in the rice fields. The day began with the *neak moulthan* or the soldiers yelling at us to get up and go to the fields. It often took me over an hour to get there with my stick, low energy and general poor health.

When I got to the fields, if we were working on irrigation infrastructure I had to sit in the mud and dig soil into a *bangki*, a two-handled basket used to move mud. Someone would then empty it elsewhere while I filled another. I could be two or three metres deep in the earth, digging and shoveling the soil. In order to do this, I had to half-crawl and half-climb into and out of the trench.

One day I remember there was heavy rain and flooding. I walked on a dyke between two flooded rice fields and stood on a piece of wood to stay out of the mud. Suddenly, I slipped off and fell into the water. Luckily someone was close by and dragged me half-out of the water so I didn't drown. No one had the strength or energy to actually lift me out.

I took time to crawl back out onto the dyke and slowly made my way home, cold and shivering. At that time living seemed no better than dying.

There was one meal break in the middle of the day, marked by the sound of two loud gongs, 15 minutes apart. We would be served one ladle of watery gruel, which may have a few grains of rice in it. This soup had already been watered down by the *neak moulthan* who poured off the richer, first broth for themselves before replacing this part with water.

This 'feeding', done in the individual labour groups, would also occur at day's end in the village, before we would lie down in a group shelter and try to sleep. Hunger made this difficult. Meetings were also held regularly after work to ensure we were 'ideologically prepared'.

The sense of isolation was compounded by the lack of trust between everyone. If someone knew something about your past, it could be used to curry favour with the *neak moulthan*, and that secret could kill. I remember in Cha Huoy there was a man who had been the director of the well-known Kosantphiep newspaper, and his wife. My mother knew him as part of her professional network in Phnom Penh. He disappeared soon after arriving, although his wife survived. Anyone who proved to be of little use in the fields similarly disappeared.

There was another form of silence, though one that we used against the *neak moulthan*. We had a saying called "*dam doeum ko*", which literally means 'plant a *ko* (or kapok) tree'. However the word '*ko*' also means mute so it actually meant 'keep quiet'. We would say it to each other if there were a *neak moulthan* or a soldier around.

The kapok tree became part of my life for other reasons. It bears large pods as 'fruit' but inside them is what looks like cotton, which is used to make stuffing for pillows. We used to eat the inside of the pods before they became fibrous and inedible. My friends say it is 'my tree'.

I was always lonely now and often scared. For a while the only other person around me was a boy in a hut next to mine. He had called out one day and cried to say his mother had just died.

His name was Chith and he was eight years old and I was 14. We became like sister and brother. He would steal rice and share it with me so I could get better. I told him not to steal, as he would get in trouble with the soldiers. Chith got caught many times and punished. They hit him hard. Every time he would have marks on his body or his face. Once they even put him in a prison.

My tears fall when I write about Chith. I didn't know how to help him and pitied him but he was so kind to me. When I had a fever he would bring me water and food and take care of me. He was like an adult but had the cheeky manner of my little brother Rathya and was so clever and not afraid of death. One day he just disappeared. I don't know to this day if Chith lived or died. After that I missed him so much.

One night I was asleep when I was woken by someone outside my hut.

"Who is there?" I called out when I was sure I wasn't dreaming.

"Laddha are you in there?" It was Wantha, and she had a friend with her.

"Wantha!" My tears came immediately. *My big sister is still alive and has come back to see me!* She pulled the cloth away from the door to the hut.

"Why do you have this cloth everywhere?" she asked me.

"To keep out the ghosts," I replied, suddenly feeling silly for having done it.

"Oh Laddha." Wantha pretended to scold me for such silliness but just touched my hair lovingly and we hugged each other tightly for a few moments. We spoke a few words but I had no energy to say any more. I had malaria and had not been able to look after myself, or my hygiene, for sometime and I smelt.

Wantha washed me a little. She gave me another pair of pants to wear. Her friend also gave me a bit of sugar cane to suck on. I guessed her friend had stolen it as things like that were never given out to us and Wantha had never stolen anything in her life. The sweet taste was so wonderful.

I knew Wantha had to leave again and I didn't ask her to stay. However, hugging my sister and talking to her again reminded me of who I was. I was Laddha, from Phnom Penh, daughter of Seng Bou and Pan SutChay, sister of Wantha and Vanna. I wasn't just a nobody working in the fields like an animal that no one cared about.

The day after Wantha visited me I had a strong fever with trembling and a headache in the late afternoon. I woke up and saw a face in front of me like that of a monkey. The creature appeared to have a naked half-man body. I was scared and told the villagers what I had seen.

"*Mit Srey*, that was '*neak ta dambauk*'. (This literally means 'the spirit of the hill.') Tell us what you saw."

In front of my hut there was a small hill. While everyone in Cambodia believes in spirits not everyone can see them. They told me it was unusual to see this spirit - that even if you prayed and wished to see him you can't. The *neak ta* spirits are everywhere and exist wherever there is a landmark or place with special features or a 'presence'.

It was another confirmation that I was someone who could see spirits, which petrified me. Rathya had died because of Khleang Meung! I was sure it meant he was coming to take my soul or at least that I was going to die as well. I could hardly breathe from the fear.

IN LATER years Wantha estimated, using information from a variety of sources and her own observations, that this creeping, unacknowledged holocaust, had had truly devastating results. Of the roughly 4,000 families dumped around Cha Huoy in late 1975, her belief was that only five or six of them had family members alive a year later. In most cases, the surviving 'families' appeared to consist of only a single person.

Because of this decimation of the population a decision was made by *Angka* to combine three villages into one. The New People that came and joined us seemed healthier and better off than we were. I thought they must have had an easier life than us. Around this time I was moved between different places according to the work the Old People wanted me to do. I worked less in the fields now and more with the less able of the New People.

When the rice harvest was taking place I worked with the old or sick women. Our job was to separate the rice grain from the husks and the rice straw.

I sat next to a stone slab and my role was to keep up regular supplies of rice to those who were grinding it to make flour, using traditional methods. There was no talking between us. We didn't know each other and did not know whom to trust, so it was better to say nothing. It was like working with mute people.

I had nowhere to stay at night as I was too far from my old hut to return each day. No one would talk to me or help me with this problem. It was now the cool season and our village was in higher country near the mountains so it was cold at night. I had no blankets and the only place to sleep was in a haystack made from the rice straw. Normally I would have been scared of the ghosts, being alone in the dark, but I couldn't sleep much and, surprisingly, they didn't bother me.

The rice straw kept me warm to some extent, but was very itchy! Late at night I would go to the *srah* (pond or dam) nearby and try and wash away the itchiness. It seemed to me I was always either cold or itchy. I also still had hemeralopia (night blindness) and at night things became blurred and I wasn't confident in recognizing what I was actually seeing. Most of the New People suffered from this condition. It meant you had to look up in order to see what was in front of you, using your peripheral vision.

It was one thing always being uncomfortable, hungry and sick with bouts of malaria and not being able to sleep. On top of this I had no one to share my misery with as no one would talk to me.

One stormy night I looked to the sky and pleaded: 'if in this world there are angels, please stop the rain now.' The rain stopped shortly after that and at the time I thought it was miraculous. I looked to the sky and thanked whoever had heard my prayer.

New People in situations similar to mine frequently looked for ways to end it all. It actually helped us cope with the threats and intimidation from the soldiers and *neak moulthan*. When dying can seem like a release from a life in hell, it loses its power to frighten.

At this time I often wanted to die. It seemed if I died no one would have noticed or cared. New People felt like we were just animals, like the cows and buffalo, but not as well fed. I also didn't know how to kill myself but I thought every day about doing it.

I lived like this for about a month before noticing two small huts some distance away. One day after work I plucked up my courage and walked close to one of the huts. There I saw an old woman who was in her fifties and had water containers that were empty in front of her hut.

"Would you like me to fill the containers for you?" I asked.

"That is very kind of you, thank you." Then she saw my walking stick. "How are you going to do that?"

"I can," I replied. I have one leg worse than the other but I have two good arms. One I use with my stick, the other I could carry water with. I took one of the containers and went to the *srah*, half-filled it and brought it back.

"What is your name, young girl?" she asked me.

"They call me *mit Srey*," I replied.

"Where do you live?"

"I sleep in the haystack, where we work. I don't have a hut."

Her name was Neak. She had noticed me living and working nearby and wondered who this girl with the awkward walk was. Neak asked me if I wanted to stay in her hut with her. There was only really room for one but she wanted to repay my kindness so I accepted and kept warm that night.

We talked, and came to like one another. I told her my real name was Laddha. She asked about my parents, and told me she had a daughter Kosany who worked in a labouring team like Wantha.

I realised then that Kosany was an old friend of Wantha's who she had met again in a meeting with the new arrivals. Kosany knew that Wantha had recognized her, and whispered to Wantha not to reveal her identity to the *neak moulthan*. She was an elite Apsara dancer who knew King Sihanouk's mother personally. This information would have spelt death for Kosany, but they never found out her secret.

Neak pitied me and told me she wanted me to look upon her as my mother. Feeling the warmth of human affection gave me some hope again and a reason to face each day. I fetched water for Neak and helped around the hut. She was not well and could not do much for herself. However, after only a week, Neak was moved, apparently to be with her other children.

Before she left, I asked her if she would help me with a problem I had worried about. I had my mother's bracelet and 14 diamonds that Wantha had given me to look after. Wantha moved around a lot, was always in rice fields or ditches and often slept where she worked. However with nowhere to live myself, I had to always keep them hidden close to me or bury them somewhere. I had done this but was anxious about forgetting where I had put them or that others might see me hiding or burying the precious items and steal them.

I asked Neak if she would look after them for me as she had a place to live and was an adult who would be more able to look after them. She said she would and so I gave them to her.

In the hut next to Neak's was a lady who I knew as *bong* Im's mother. Im was also in one of the labouring teams. When Neak moved away, Im's mother said I could sleep in her hut. I assumed this was just kindness but soon found out she had other motives.

Im's mother had heard about the diamonds and thought that I would give them to her for showing me the kindness of a place to sleep. When she found out that I had given them to Neak to keep for me, her kindness vanished and she made me sleep on a bamboo bed outside her hut. Although she did lend me her mosquito net, I was back to being cold.

Luckily I found some charcoal under the house, so decided to try and warm myself at night with it. I put some of the charcoal and some wood in a bowl and, using a match that *bong* Im's mother had found, lit a fire. It was late and it worked all right the first night. I curled up under my mosquito net close to the fire and the hut, and got a better night's sleep.

The next night I repeated this and was close to falling asleep when I heard someone brush against the thatched wall of the hut. It was Im's mother

"What are you doing you silly girl," she yelled at me. "You can't light a fire. You might burn down the hut or melt the mosquito net."

"But I am so cold," I said, feeling guilty.

"If the *neak moulthan* find out, they will punish you." It was true that it was against the rules for people to do anything like this on their own without permission. But it was late at night and everyone was asleep and I was frozen.

She soon complained about what I had done to the *neak moulthan* but, rather than getting in trouble, I was given a small hut to live in nearby. After this I was moved to other areas and thankfully my day-to-day life became less difficult.

I was told to work with the older *neak moulthan* - the Grandma *moulthan* - and help them with cooking. I wasn't allowed near the food but would fetch water or firewood and also water the vegetable garden we all needed to survive.

The women were all about 60 or more and so, being the only young person there, I was useful to them. Despite being one of the New People, the old grandmas actually grew to like me because I was hard working and didn't complain.

From morning until noon I would find wood for the grandma *moulthan* to cook with, but in the afternoon I was relatively free. One day, as we were all resting from the heat, I noticed that one of the old women had some grey hairs in her head. As she was drifting off to sleep, I tweaked some of these grey hairs out with my finger-nails. I had learnt how to do this from Mum when she sat in our

hammock in front of the garage. The other old women saw this and
made me do it for them too. The rice soup I was given after that was
a little thicker than before.

11

RATS AND "RABBITS"

AN IMPORTANT reason I survived the killing fields of Cha Huoy was because of a lady called Phi Sa Em, but who we knew as '*mae srey*'. She had a husband, Juep Song, and a daughter living with her there. Husbands and wives were not allowed to sleep together, but had to live, eat and work in different groups.

Sa Em and Song were very resourceful people. Through them we learnt how to catch rats. At times when we thought we could get away with it - after work - we would locate rat holes in the fields.

Rat holes usually have two openings and we would pour water into one and wait at the other to catch them as they tried to escape. We would pounce on them, smash their head on a rock, cut off their heads and keep the rest until it could be cooked safely – usually much later at night. We would skin them, roll them in salt and fry them – *chngan nah!* (very tasty)

Song would also set traps at night to catch rats. Sa Em told us that if we had known them earlier they could have saved our mother and brothers. Song could catch seven or eight rats on a single expedition. Sa Em believed if they hadn't eaten rats, they would not have survived either. They would also steal food and rice for me. Sa Em would also carry me to meals and, because she arrived a little late, end up with the most diluted gruel herself for this kindness to me.

Wantha warned me against eating rats as, having some medical knowledge, she thought they could make me go blind. At the time I had blood in my tears, and was suffering from conjunctivitis. It was quite common among New People, and someone suggested rubbing chili into my eyes. I was quite worried about going blind so I did this and it helped me recover from this condition. Despite my hunger I did not eat much of it, only tasting rat meat once or twice. This was very difficult for me. To a starving person, the smell of salted meat cooking is almost irresistible.

SA EM, like me, was employed in one of the kitchens around Cha Huoy or the village next door, Ampil Choung. Despite her willingness to take risks she was trusted enough to actually cook food (with the obvious temptation to eat some when no one was looking). In addition to gathering, cooking and watering, she sometimes had to take the food out to teams working in the fields. In this way she witnessed another part of the horror that was taking place in our region in 1978.

Once at this time, I saw trucks loaded up with young, fair-skinned people. I found out later they were ethnic Vietnamese people from Svay Rieng and Prey Veng, two provinces that form the border with Vietnam. It was strange. They wore beautiful, new black cloth and were of a paler complexion than us. The group I saw all seemed to be young - teenagers rather than adults.

I heard the grandma *moulthan* murmuring and talking quietly with each other and with the soldier who drove the cow cart. I heard them talking about rabbits, white and naked in a deep hole. In each hole there were 20 or 30 rabbits. As the soldier walked past me I asked him, "Why don't you bring these rabbits to the village so we can eat them. They are delicious and we are all so hungry."

"Do you want to be a rabbit? Maybe it is time for you to go there with me," the soldier replied. I didn't know what he meant.

"Leave her alone," one of the grandma *moulthan* said to him. "She works hard and is helpful to us in preparing the food."

The soldier looked at me and shrugged his shoulders and went back to his ox cart. Soon after that I saw all the black clothes being brought back by the soldiers to the village to be shared with the grandma *moulthan*.

Sa Em had to take the lunch out one day to the leader of a team. As she approached him and the soldiers around him, she suddenly noticed that there was a large hole in front of them, full of naked, dead bodies. This was the final resting place for the teenagers I had seen in the truck and hadn't been covered over yet.

These poor children had been caught up in the paranoid machinations of Pol Pot and his cronies. They ended their life a long way from home with no idea what they had done to deserve this fate.

Sa Em ran away when she saw the legs and arms and bloodied heads in the pit. She vomited and tried to put it out of her head. The leader warned her to keep quiet about what she had seen or she would end up the same way.

SA EM had to work in the kitchen as long as there was work to be done there. She often worked late into the night because of a soldier we came across before - *mit* Tang.

"I am bringing back a frog to cook. Don't go to sleep," Tang would tell Sa Em.

Tang, and other *mit yeung*, walked out each afternoon into the rice fields and selected that day's victims - New People who had offended *Angka* in some way. All eyes would follow them. Once chosen, the trembling men and women would have their arms hog-tied behind their back by these soldiers and be lead away. Maybe they would be taken to a prison to be tortured then killed or just killed straight away. They never came back.

As Sa Em waited in the kitchen as the night closed in, she knew what was going to happen. It was just a matter of how many she would have to cook this time. Tang and his fellow executioners would cut the livers out of their victims, either before or after killing them. After burying the bodies, the soldiers would bring the livers back for Sa Em to cook. Most days there would be four or five. Some days there would even be a whole *bangki* full of them. Tang would bring his axe with him, rub it on Sa Em's shoulder and stand behind her as she cooked this 'food'.

"Would your liver be as tasty as these frogs," he would taunt. "You should eat some." Sa Em always refused. She said he ate so many livers his eyes became increasingly yellow.

However, despite his horrific acts, as mentioned earlier, *mit* Tang was to become part of the reason Wantha and I did not die over her refusal to marry.

The issue came to a head one day when everyone was called to a public meeting in the village. There would have been over 1,000 people there. I was absent, but Wantha was present, along with the rest of her *chalat*. *Mit* Pet knew that Wantha was to be executed and made an example of at this meeting. What happened next was so miraculous and bizarre, I still find it hard to believe.

The meeting heard that *mit* Tang had been found to be having sex with one of the New People and this could not be overlooked. *Mit* Tang and the unfortunate woman were tied together, publicly humiliated, denounced and taken away. We never saw Tang again. The Khmer Rouge regularly killed their own, so it is likely that Tang was executed.

After this revelation and judgment, everyone at the meeting was told to go back to where they were working which Wantha, and the hundreds of others, did with relief. Somebody later remembered about Wantha and her supposed fate, but by then no one knew where to find her. Wantha found this out much later when she ran into the soldier who had supposedly been looking for her off and on for months. By then it seemed things had changed and the local *mit yeung* had lost interest in killing Wantha for her refusal to marry.

If there is such a thing as karma, then this is surely an example of it. Sa Em, Song, their daughter and Wantha all survived the Khmer Rouge nightmare, but Tang did not.

I like to think the goodness of Sa Em in the end was stronger than the cruel, insane morality of the Khmer Rouge. Murdering and disemboweling innocent victims day-in day-out is okay, but having sex without permission is a capital offence.

THE MASSACRE of the Vietnamese civilians living close to the border by the Khmer Rouge was yet another murderous, vengeful and futile act in the death throes of a regime whose time was up.

Many Cambodians living in that region had fled to neighboring Vietnam as it became clear that Pol Pot was lashing out at anyone imagined to be disloyal, or whose name had been offered by the victims of torture at Tuol Sleng. It was anyone's guess who would be next.

As the result of Vietnam becoming a refuge, Pol Pot also needlessly provoked Vietnam by venturing into their territory and killing civilians. In December 1978, this unnecessary and suicidal folly resulted in Vietnam invading Cambodia and, within days, taking control of Phnom Penh. By January, the Khmer Rouge no longer ruled Cambodia. They fled to the mountainous western border with Thailand – unfortunately exactly where we were!

Wantha, Sa Em and her family and I were often separated over the last two years of the Khmer Rouge nightmare, being sent to work in different areas. Because of our poor health, and the ever-present reality that we could be arrested and killed, we never knew when, or if, we would see each other again.

One day I saw some of the *grandma moulthan* wrapping their clothes and being told they were being moved to another village, in the mountains. I was told to get my things and sit in the cow cart as well so I complied.

"Where are we going?" I asked. They shook their head - nobody knew, or they weren't telling me if they did. Our cart headed west and, after several kilometres, started to climb up the valley towards the nearest mountain. I looked at the trees and thought nature was very beautiful. I don't know what time of day it was but the clouds started to come across the sun and it became dark.

Then by chance I saw a group of women walking in a line about 50 metres away from us. There were about 30 or 40 of them and they were carrying bags of salt up the mountain. I looked hard and thought I saw a woman who looked like Wantha. I jumped up.

"Sister, sister Wantha" I yelled out loudly. It was Wantha and she turned and looked but wasn't sure it was me. We hadn't seen each other for nearly two years. Dropping her bag of salt she ran to me, stood in front of the cart and asked the soldiers to stop. Wantha has always had a presence and the soldiers did as she asked.

"This is my sister," she said to the younger soldier, pointing to me. "Can she please come with me?"

"If she stays with you how can she get rice for eating?" he grumpily replied.

"I can share mine with her," Wantha replied. "I have not seen my sister for two years. Please can you let her come with me, *mit*. I will look after her. She can work with me."

The soldiers were not used to having to argue with New People like this and Wantha once again had taken a big risk. However I think she knew she would probably never see me again if she couldn't take me with her this time.

Wantha also knew she had the respect of her leaders because of her hard work. In addition, it was perhaps a sign that things had changed and that there had been a shift in relations between the Old and New People. Compassion was not a trait encouraged by the Khmer Rouge.

"We have said you can't take her. We have our orders - now go away! You have left your team."

Wantha moved to the other, older soldier and continued to plead with him. She has always been a strong and assertive person. She didn't insult or get angry with them or cause them to lose face. But she wasn't going to leave me. Eventually the older soldier relented.

"I don't care too much if we leave her with her sister. Other soldiers will soon come and sort them out."

My sister thanked him and he signaled for me to get down from the cart. Wantha helped me to come off the cart, which then started up again and moved away. I looked at the women still sitting on the cart. One waved to me. She looked so sad.

Wantha held my hand and we walked slowly away. She carried me some of the way and we both tried to ignore the sound of wild dogs close by. Her work team had arrived back at their camp near the mountain well before us. By the time we joined them it was getting dark and they scolded my sister for being late. The work team hadn't kept any rice soup for us so we were very hungry. I felt sorry for my sister who suffered in this way because of me.

SUCH WAS our isolation from everything beyond our village that we had no idea the Khmer Rouge regime had been replaced, even several months after its downfall. Only a few days after Wantha picked me from the ox-cart - it would have been around June 1979 - we realized that the *neak moulthan* were becoming less interested in us, and seemed to be making themselves scarce. This was confirmed when one day we saw an ox-cart next to a hut with no one in charge of it. This was prize property for powerful, village-level *neak moulthan* and there it was, just sitting there with nobody owning it.

When we decided to take the ox-cart to go back to Cha Huoy, no one stopped us. What could this mean? On arrival in the village, we found there were only New People - and Vietnamese soldiers.

Khmer Rouge were lying dead in the rice fields and tracks. Bodies in black pajamas lay in pools of blood, dispatched by knives, rocks, anything to get some revenge.

The Khmer Rouge regime had lasted three years, eight months and twenty days but for us, it was over four years. However, the nightmare was finally over and we had both survived.

12

WHERE TO NOW?

'Who am I? What is real? Why have I survived? Could my father still be alive? Who should I be afraid of? Will the Vietnamese soldiers look after us? Where will our food come from now? All these questions I didn't know the answer to.

'What do I know? I have Wantha who I know would never leave or betray me. I know that Neak and Kosany, and Sa Em, are good people and we can again trust each other. It feels right to be friendly and smile at others, and not be suspicious of everyone. The bad people have been killed or have run away. That feels right as well.'

'When I last had some control over my life I was 13, in awe of my parents and surrounded by a loving, omnipresent family. Since then I have had to hide and ignore every impulse that arose in my head or my heart. I had lived in fear of dying every day, and watched my family and many, many others die or disappear. I was 18 now, orphaned, but despite everything, alive.'

It took some time to realize that I was now in charge of my own destiny. Wantha was 29, and my rock. She had been her own person since her late teens, and had, despite events, resisted the Khmer Rouge. Her refusal to agree to their forced marriage undoubtedly kept that independent flame in her burning through the dark days of the Pol Pot regime. There was a bridge too far that she had not crossed, even under threat of execution. For many thousands of New

People their 'bridge too far' had cost them their life. Wantha and I did not have to pay that price.

But Wantha's resistance was not a foolhardy one. Her clever 'dance' with Pet kept the enemy close and comfortable. The small concessions by Pet of extra rice or some pumpkin that were gratefully accepted by Wantha, gave Pet a chance to feel like she was Wantha's equal. For this illiterate, ordinary villager, to believe she could keep smart, strong, and useful Wantha in orbit around her made Pet powerful and confident amongst the other *neak moulthan*. The 'dance' the two of them had done around each other had probably ended up saving the lives of them both.

For all of us who were left, the shine of freedom was tarnished by the loss of loved ones. The exhilaration of still being alive while the Khmer Rouge were banished soon gave way to the sadness of loss, and the wondering - why me? Why am I left alive?

The Vietnamese soldiers provided Cambodians some reassurance that anarchy was not imminent, especially when compared to what had gone before. For a while they helped make food available to us, and we could go where we wanted. However to suddenly have such unbounded freedom was paralysing.

The first thing to come into focus was how to feed ourselves. This ultimately meant making a decision about where to go. This village had been our prison and had nothing left for us.

In Cambodia we have a saying: "Once them, once us". It means the fear and intimidation that had been inflicted on us would now be reversed. Those of the old regime would now know that fear.

Wantha felt indebted to Pet in some way. The bond forged the night when Pet told Wantha she was to be killed, and that even she, *chalat* leader Pet, could not stop it, still held. Wantha could see what would happen to Khmer Rouge leaders and soldiers and agreed to protect her old *chalat* leader and her family.

Keeping her out of the hands of vengeful New People would not be easy, given Pet's high profile as a *neak moulthan* leader. Everyone knew Pet and wanted her dead.

Travelling on the highway would have meant running into New

People so that wasn't possible for Pet. Another way was needed.

We agreed to meet them in Maung Russei and we would stand by them as long as needed. Wantha and I would travel there by National Road # 5, along with a friend from Wantha's *chalat*, a young woman called Srey Ny and her mother. Meanwhile, Pet's family - herself, her husband and their two teenage daughters - would travel to Maung Russei by the back roads, tracks, and forest.

In truth there was another thread to this decision to prolong our stay in the province. Wantha was grieving our lost family. In fact we were all in mourning. Emotions had no place in Khmer Rouge society but now that we were free to feel what we wanted, what we felt was extreme grief.

Neak had kept our jewelry safe and, when returning it, she and Kosany had asked us to come back to Phnom Penh with them. Wantha said there was now nothing there for us as our parents and brothers were all dead. Whilst I would have been happy to go back to the city, most of all I wanted to do whatever Wantha thought best. And so late one night we headed off along the same track we had arrived on, all those years ago …

SOME DAYS later we found a place to live in the district of Maung Russei, about 25 kilometres closer to Battambang, and started to plan a settled existence. Pet's family arrived and we hid them from public view, denying to anyone who asked that they were with us. We told them we hadn't seen Pet but that she was one of the nicer, more forgivable, *neak moulthan*.

We lived with Pet's family for several months and gradually the national mood for revenge subsided. Instead, people now were consumed by the constant struggle to find a way to get food where none was available easily. Starvation loomed as a real threat, with a broken farming system and few people planning as far ahead as the next crop. Wantha and Srey Ny took the ox cart wherever they thought they could find something to eat.

Pet's family were not much help at subsistence living or growing rice. They knew little about rice farming and made little effort to learn. The daughters sat around and the father, Phun, blamed others for their situation and did almost nothing to change it. They seemed content with relying on Wantha and Srey Ny to meet their needs.

Wantha has never suffered fools gladly and did not think much of Phun.

"You stay in bed until eight o'clock. You need to be up at 4 o'clock to plant the rice. It isn't hot then," she would admonish Phun. "The day is too hot now and there are other things that need to be done."

Wantha wasn't worried about Phun losing face, and Pet agreed with Wantha. She knew her husband was a liability. He couldn't grow rice, and would sit around with his daughters, waiting for others to take the initiative.

The chronic shortage of rice and other foods dominated everyone's thinking. There was also the fear of another, foreign, communist regime taking over, motivating many to risk their life and try to escape Cambodia.

Hundreds of thousands of desperate survivors headed for the Thai border with whatever valuables they had able to hide over the last four years. Gold and diamonds would be exchanged for food or a dangerous, guided walk through the jungle to Thailand. This had become the new currency in the absence of any viable paper money.

Wantha began to consider going to the Thai border. She had heard that people didn't stay there but could transfer to other countries through the Red Cross. However, I couldn't walk that far and it was a very dangerous journey for anyone, with remnants of the Khmer Rouge and bandits still around.

No one really knew what was happening or how to get there. Wantha wanted to find out more.

One day she said to Pet: "I want to find out what is at the border. There are camps there we can go to but we need to find out more about them first."

"Don't go there, Wantha," Pet said. "We need you here. We would be worried without you. Also you are a woman and might not be safe."

"We can't just try to live here. We will starve if we don't do something else," Wantha replied.

"Why doesn't Phun go instead of you," Pet said. She thought that Wantha might not come back so this was Pet's way of keeping her. "He is a man and if you give him some of the diamonds he may be able to find out about the camps. He can handle the rough trip and the danger. He can also bring back some rice for us all."

Despite misgivings, Wantha agreed that Phun could go, taking with him our mother's 14-diamond pendant that we had kept hidden for so long. We were starving and it was the only currency we had.

Phun headed off one morning with the last of our wealth, and the responsibility to give us all some direction in an increasingly desperate plight. He went to Or Crew, a place on the border where trading took place. Food trickled in from Thailand and gold and diamonds trickled back the other way.

When Phun returned several days later, we could see immediately he had almost nothing to show for his trip. When he arrived, his eyes would not meet ours and he could only talk of excuses. He carried a little bread, but had traded 9 of the 14 diamonds.

We were all disappointed but Pet was furious and screamed at him. He seemed to have been eating well himself but forgotten about us who were starving.

Tensions rose between us. We still didn't know how to get to Thailand but knew that I couldn't attempt a journey that meant walking a long way. We couldn't go to Phnom Penh because of Pet's Khmer Rouge background, and anyway we didn't know how to get there. We knew there would be trucks but they charged for that trip and we had little left to offer.

However, doing nothing wasn't an option. We had no food to speak of and the next rice harvest was months away. If we stayed there we would starve. Wantha and I now had time to consider what we really wanted to do. Maybe Vanna was back home? Maybe Seurn and his family had survived. How would Chittra find us? The pull of the family had worked its way back into our hearts and got stronger each day.

Wantha struggled with this dilemma for some time and it got harder and harder to find food. Srey Ny and her mother wanted to go to Phnom Penh and find their family. We all talked about how to find our way there and gradually started to come up with a plan.

One morning, several months now after we had left Cha Huoy, Wantha spoke to Pet.

"We must return to Phnom Penh to find who is left from our family," she said. "It is safe for you to go back to Cha Huoy now. All the people who want to hurt you have left."

"My husband cannot protect or look after me and our family," she cried. "We need you, Wantha! Don't leave us! Can we come with you?"

"If you come to Phnom Penh there are people there that will still want to kill you because of your past. I will come and visit you when I find my relatives. I have paid back your good deed."

"You know we saved your life when the New People wanted to kill you," Wantha continued. "They could have killed us as well but we saved you. We have no diamonds left, we have protected you, but now we must go."

Pet was quiet, just crying. Wantha went on speaking.

"Between you and me I think we do not owe each other anything now. I will always remember for the rest of my life that you saved us. Now we are going home."

Srey Ny and Wantha loaded us on to the ox-cart straight away and we left. I was stunned that the break had happened so quickly but Wantha did not want to give Pet any time to change our decision. We rode the cart out and headed for the main road - National Road # 5.

WE DIDN'T try to get to Phnom Penh straight away. Surviving each day was still our only focus. The four of us - Wantha, Srey Ny, her mother and I - did not have enough food so we pushed on, sleeping in the cart and resting when we could.

Some days later, as the dark clouds threatened to soak us again we reached the main road. The lightning frightened me, and I was worrying about getting drenched when suddenly a voice rang out from near our cart.

"Sister Wantha, sister Wantha." We all looked round and saw a pretty young woman on a bike coming towards us.

"Ouk! How wonderful to see you," said Wantha. She jumped down from the cart and the two women hugged each other. They had spent two years together in the *chalat* and had a special bond.

"What are you doing here, Wantha?" she asked. "I thought you went back to Phnom Penh after the Vietnamese freed us."

"It is a long story, Ouk. We have no water or food or any place to shelter. Can you help us?"

"Of course, Wantha. I live here. Come with me and we will look after you and hear your story." She then introduced herself to the rest of us and took us to where she stayed.

Ouk was a Laotian, as was her husband, who spoke a bit less Khmer than his outgoing wife. They had lived in the area since leaving Cha Huoy and managed to find enough sustenance to survive for the moment. We were given a small hut nearby to shelter in and stay for the few days we planned to stay. The next step was to push on to Battambang, to see my mother's relatives. I was glad to have found shelter but was scared of the Vietnamese soldiers who also stayed in Ouk's village as well. I only knew bad things about soldiers with guns.

The hut we stayed in was part of a pagoda called "Soriya". The pagoda covered a large area, maybe 100 metres by 100 metres, and had a large concrete pond, as well as other stupas and *wats* (temples) There were Vietnamese soldiers everywhere.

Despite our original plan only to stay for a few days, Wantha was very quickly drafted into being chief of security for the village, which was known as Kea 3. In a very short time she moved up to being the secretary of the Maung Russei District Committee, at the time an important role as the government was still in flux.

The main issues for the community were security and food. We learnt that the Khmer Rouge were still active in the area, living in the jungle some 25 or 30 kilometres away, and creeping out to kidnap people, steal rice and cause trouble. They had explosives, forcing us to hide when they attacked. The Vietnamese soldiers were an insurance of sorts but we wanted to make our own decisions and look after ourselves. Young Cambodians acted as guards at night, and distributed food fairly, based on what people needed as well as how much they contributed to the community.

We ran out of food all the time. When this happened we would organise a foraging trip to the mountains to bring back whatever we could find. Fifty of us would take ten ox-carts. We found cucumbers, watermelons, and other vegetables. Once we ran into some Khmer Rouge who ran away, maybe because of our numbers. In a reminder of what we had lived through, at their camp we found human livers being cooked. We also found a gun they had abandoned, which we brought back to our village.

However, gradually Wantha's and my thoughts turned again to getting back to Phnom Penh to find any surviving relatives.

Each week Red Cross trucks drove past our pagoda, bringing rice and supplies from Phnom Penh to Battambang. These trucks returned empty, so there was plenty of room to take people in them. However the drivers charged for this service. It took gold or diamonds to buy you a trip to the city.

My last possession of any worth was some gold flake from the covering of the Buddhist statues that my brothers and I had been given by our mother, but Ouk said we must keep that out of respect for the Buddha. In total, between us, we only had two chi (about 50 grams) of gold. A ride to Phnom Penh was three chi per person.

However, a plan took shape. Firstly, Ouk decided she could use her female charms to convince the driver to take her and Wantha as passengers. One evening Wantha returned to our hut, bristling with excitement.

"Ouk and I are going to catch a ride on a truck tomorrow," she said. Then she slowed down a little and explained the rest of the plan.

"I'll go home and find out who is alive. I will come back for you as soon as I can. Wait with Srey Ny's mother and the children. Look after them." Ouk's husband also stayed behind in the pagoda.

Early the next morning Ouk came past and Wantha crept out to meet her without waking me. Over the next few days I became agitated with the roller coaster of emotions flooding through me. I could be going back to my childhood home ... back to what I knew... back to learning again? But Mum and Dad and my brothers would not be there now or ever again. But what about Vanna, Sareth and their children? And darling Noem and her children? Would any of them still be alive?

About a week later Wantha arrived back with Ouk, and she had answers to most of those questions.

13

THE RECKONING

OF ALL those who had lived in the house by the canal in Phnom Penh, the first to return was *bong* Seurn, my older male cousin who had lifted me on his shoulders to the acupuncture clinic. We had last seen him just after the evacuation at Prek Eng. He had found his way there with his wife and three children and sensed the hatred the Khmer Rouge had for former Lon Nol officials and military policemen like himself. He had to decide if his family were better off with or without him – just as Father had to decide which family he would stay with.

Seurn decided to head for Touk Meas, where people were less likely to know about his role as a military policeman. He rode there and left his family in the care of his wife's relations. His father also travelled to Touk Meas, but met the same fate as my father, being taken to a forested area a few kilometres out of town and executed soon after arriving. Seurn was soon accused of being a 'three star' - a lieutenant general - in the military and arrested. He was taken to a prison in a remote area of Takeo province.

In his prison, each Friday a truck would roll up and deliver another batch of prisoners, and would take away a similar number. Under Pol Pot to be imprisoned was to be deemed guilty, to then be tortured and finally executed.

In a strange turn of events, Seurn avoided this fate because of a falling out between two leaders in the prison. The Khmer Rouge official who wanted Seurn dead - the more senior of the two - was himself taken away and replaced by the other.

For some reason this man was not convinced of Seurn's guilt, so Seurn stayed out of the Friday truck routine. After eight months, he was released from the prison and sent to work on a plantation nearby. However his good luck did run out. He later found that his family had perished, with his wife and three children, dying of disease and starvation.

Once the regime was swept away and he was released, Seurn returned to Phnom Penh and went straight to our family's house. He found five families already living there and knew there was nothing he could do about that.

The new residents told Seurn that the house had been filled with medical supplies by the Khmer Rouge during their rule. It was close to Tuol Sleng, my old high school, and the main prison and torture centre of the regime. Our house had probably been used by the soldiers and party functionaries while the atrocities were being carried out in Tuol Sleng.

Seurn realized he could not evict the families now living in our house, as after the regime collapse it had become a matter of 'first in, first served', with property. The Khmer Rouge had destroyed land titles, killed most of the owners of the properties and there was no police force to enforce any laws in any case. Who was to say who really owned anything any more? For those who returned first, they could help themselves to whatever they could grab and defend.

Seurn managed to get a job driving buses in the capital and was given an apartment in Borey Keyla by his new government employers. He had also found a new partner who had lost touch with her husband, and they moved in and set up house together.

One day Seurn had a bright idea and returned to our old home. He asked the families there if he could write something on the wall, which would allow any of our returning family members to find him. The families agreed so he scrawled the Borey Keyla address on the wall and this became the key to reuniting the family members. Of course, at this time Seurn had no idea who, if anyone, was still alive.

When Wantha came back from Maung Russei with Ouk, she went to our old house and found Seurn's message. Wantha wrote on the wall that she and I had survived and then went to find the address Seurn had written. It was 7 January, 1980, the first anniversary of the overthrow of the Pol Pot regime. There were celebrations of sorts and Seurn was not at home when Wantha and Ouk arrived. They had to wait outside as his new partner's mother did not know them and would not let her come in.

When Seurn saw Wantha he ran to hug and hold her. In his arms Wantha shook and started to cry as all the grief and sadness that had dammed up inside her for the last four years flooded out in tears. She struggled to find any words. How can you talk about events that are too painful to even think about? How do you tell a loved one that his sister is dead?

Gradually the shaking subsided and Wantha steeled herself and began to tell the story. Firstly, she told of Prey Veng Pong Tek and Dad's execution. Then she told of Cha Huoy, and the extinction of our mother and brothers - and finally of the death of Prong, Seurn's sister.

Seurn had already had to bear the news that he had lost his own children and wife. Now he had to go through a similar pain again. Somehow he managed to listen to Wantha's story to the end and then they hugged each other very tightly.

Both Seurn and Wantha knew that such chronic pain could not be handled by them talking, which left the awful events of the last four years exposed again like a raw nerve. I believe both Seurn and Wantha left this meeting knowing they simply could not have another conversation like this, as it would destroy their ability to function normally. Their pain had to be put away, so they could move on and start again.

They had both survived, and knew that the family was now in their hands. But who was left to look after? Seurn told Wantha to go back and get me from Maung Russei, and we would all live together with him in Borey Keyla.

Wantha and Ouk then went to find out about Ouk's family, but no one was left alive. Some days later, the two women got a ride back to Maung Russei and, after some difficulty in securing a space on a truck, we were all on our way back to Phnom Penh.

WE WERE dropped off in front of the train station in Phnom Penh in the afternoon. Srey Ny's mum asked me to wait there with her daughters and our belongings. She was going to get her older male cousin to come and pick me up.

I looked around and could not recognise Phnom Penh. There were very few people walking around, no cars or motorcycles. The streets were dirty and looked like they had been abandoned for years, which of course they had been. When I was young I watched a Dracula movie in the Kirirom Cinema and it had been set in a place like this - a ghost town.

Suddenly a man on a pushbike approached me. There was a contraption behind his bike, which I hadn't seen before.

"Where do you want to go?" he asked me. "How do you know me?", I said. He asked me if I was new to Phnom Penh and I said I was. He just laughed and rode away. I still didn't know what he had wanted and was worried as I didn't feel safe, especially with the other girls to look after.

I found out later he was asking me if I wanted to pay for a lift to my home. They had things called *kang dops*, instead of cyclos. These inventions carry people and things behind a motorbike. The old cyclos were pushbikes with a big seat in front of the rider usually used to carry people.

At that time in Phnom Penh we had to pay for rides in uncooked rice, rather than money, which was still non-existent. The government did not have enough money to pay salaries so rice was used as it had become as precious as gold. Everyone thought I was silly for not knowing what was going on when the driver had approached me.

The day after meeting Seurn, Wantha and he went to see Seylo, who had also survived. Seylo had never wanted to mix with our family but Wantha thought she should try and meet and share stories of what had happened. Seylo had stayed near Prek Eng and, although surviving, had lost five of her children. Only the two youngest were still alive: Sakvaney and Kessaney, who had been born during the Khmer Rouge regime.

Seylo told Wantha that she wanted to organise for a monk to perform a ceremony in memory of my father, who of course was also the father of her children. Unfortunately Seylo then became quite nasty to Wantha, whom she blamed for changing my father's mind that day on the bus near Prek Eng and taking him away from her and their family.

"If your father had stayed with me he would not have been killed," Seylo said. "He would have been safe with me, but you could not protect him." This was obviously not true but Wantha was deeply hurt by this accusation and she has never forgotten it.

Wantha also found out that Noem was still alive. Noem had gone from Prek Eng to Kampong Cham province, north-east of Phnom Penh, but had then been moved to Pursat province, where she was now living. She had also written on the wall of our old house.

Again, the good news and the bad news were wrapped up in the same moment. The joy of Noem's survival was tempered by the fact that, of the 6 children she took from Prek Eng, only one remained alive. It was mum's favourite little girl, Sopheavy, who was now 11 years old. My two half siblings, Sokuntheary (Noem's daughter) and Seilakvatei, (Seylo's daughter) who had been closest in age to me and who had received the same birthday presents, were both dead.

Wantha went to Pursat and collected Noem and her daughter and they joined us at Borey Keyla. Dara, my older half-sister, who had been brought as a baby to our doorstep, also wrote to us to tell us she and her two children were alive. She had a boy, seven years old and a girl five years old. Her husband had been a Military Policeman like Seurn, and had been killed in the first wave of executions, leaving Dara to bring up her two children alone.

And what of my oldest sister Vanna?

The people who now stayed in our old house told us that a 'strange woman', about the age of Vanna, had come to the house and told them she was the "first child of the owner". That was all she would say. She cried and cried then left and did not leave a message on the wall.

However, we soon heard more information about Vanna from her husband's relatives who lived with her during the Pol Pot regime. One, who had lost her husband and four children, told us that Vanna's husband Sareth had been taken away in the same way as Dad and had never been seen again. Vanna had pleaded with the soldiers to be allowed to go with him but was not allowed.

In her grief at losing her husband, and with the prospect of a future of work in the swampy rice fields, with little food or medicine for her children, Vanna had lost her mind. She killed her children with a knife, and then tried to take her own life by cutting her throat. However, others intervened, took Vanna to a hospital and saved her life.

In the years to come we tried to contact Vanna telling her we were alive. We put notices in the newspaper and even on the television. We said we are still alive and please get in contact if you have survived.

My belief is that Vanna had arrived back at the old family home and saw the names on the wall, which did not include any of her full siblings, as Wantha had not arrived there yet. As a result she may have assumed we were all dead.

Vanna did not get along with her half siblings and so maybe just felt without hope. The "strange" lady that day told the family that she was going back to Battambang and we tried, through mum's relatives there, to search for her but to no avail. Although I believe she survived Pol Pot, we will probably never know for sure. The uncertainty continues to haunt us to this day.

When the Khmer Rouge were defeated by the Vietnamese liberators there was huge international interest in what had happened, and what was going to happen. Many survivors decided that they wanted to escape what had become a war-ravaged wasteland by fleeing to Thailand and from there onto third countries, like France, Australia or the USA. Very soon, refugee camps were set up by the United

Nations and Red Cross to protect and process the large numbers of people trying to escape from Cambodia.

Chittra had stayed in Paris after flying out of Phnom Penh in the days before Pol Pot took over. He joined dad's two sisters, Thay and Heng, who had married French nationals in the 1950's and settled back in France. These women had been trying for years to get other family members out of Cambodia - especially Dad and his immediate family. Aunty Thay had paid for Ratana and Wantha to fly out in 1975, but of course they didn't make it.

Now, in 1979, with Pol Pot gone, and news everywhere of the catastrophic legacy left by the Khmer Rouge, efforts to repatriate family members went into full swing again.

At the time Cambodia was still communist, even if the Khmer Rouge had been defeated. There was limited freedom and if anyone were caught trying to leave they would be arrested and put in prison. With the conditions in jail, this effectively amounted to a death sentence - 'killing without a weapon' - so it was difficult to plan and arrange an escape. It would also have meant a dangerous journey through forests with landmines, bandits and Khmer Rouge guerillas, who were still waging war on civilians and Vietnamese and Khmer soldiers.

Aunty Thay and her husband found work with the Red Cross and went to the border camps as volunteers and worked with refugees. They were hoping to find out about family members who had survived and get them out. To that end they also employed a very young and resourceful boy of about 12 years old to come into Cambodia to find us and arrange for us to escape through Poipet, on the Thai border. Thay spent a lot of money on this as she was determined to help her brother's children.

As you can imagine, with my difficulty in walking it would have been impossible for me to think about escaping. Wantha knew that and told Thay in a letter that she could not leave me behind. Because the others relied so much on Wantha they would not go either.

Thay did not really appreciate this situation and so became angry that no one would leave after she had spent so much money and time trying to get us out. I felt she blamed me for this situation and I knew that if it was not for me they might all have been able to leave. Chittra, who had been living with them since leaving in 1975, fell out with Thay over this and moved out of their house.

I felt guilty and could not sleep knowing everyone wanted to leave Cambodia. One evening when we were all going out to have a meal with friends I said I was sick and stayed home. When they left, I found a bottle full of tablets and swallowed them all. I simply could not live with the knowledge that I was to blame for their situation.

When they came home Wantha found me, realized what had happened and I was rushed to the hospital where she worked. The medical staff saved my life. Wantha told me off and said I must not do that again. Some time later she suggested that I should change my name. I had been given the name Laddha for a very specific reason and now I should explain why.

My maternal grandfather, Naow Pan, had three children with Yaem, his *de facto* partner who loved to gamble. There were two boys and a girl. The girl was Sokhom, with whom we had stayed at Prek Eng, after the evacuation. One of Yaem's sons was a man called Pan Ottdom. Mother got on well with him and he was a highly regarded teacher who taught in Battambang.

Around 1960 Ottdam came to know an attractive young colleague called Laddha. She fell in love with him and got to know mother, who wanted them to marry as she loved Laddha very much. However Ottdom wasn't interested and spurned her advances.

Laddha was so upset at this unrequited love that she swallowed a bottle of tablets and killed herself. A few days before this Mum had dreamt that Laddha had asked her if she could come and stay with our family and Mum had agreed. The next day Mum, who was pregnant with me at the time, found out Laddha was dead.

To a devout Buddhist like my mother there was profound significance in all these events. She interpreted them to mean that I was to be the reincarnation of Laddha and so when I was born shortly after, I was given the name.

When I too tried to take my own life, Wantha said the name

Laddha had come to be associated with suicide and I should change it. I agreed and so from that day became Addheka. This name has a meaning for me to do with love.

As I have said, my aunt in France was upset to hear that we were staying put and lost interest in us after that. However, Chittra decided that he still wanted to rescue father's offspring from the communist regime and worked overtime to raise the money to do that.

Seylo, who had survived with her two children and her sister, let Chittra know that she wanted them all out and implored him to make that happen. He was torn, as he wanted to help his own siblings but could not stand by when he could save the life of the two young girls.

Seylo eventually left the country on a passport with my mother's name on it. She was Pan SutChay when she left Cambodia.

Picture taken in 1980, with Wantha, dark shirt and me to her left.

The house by the canal, taken around 1970.
Vanna is with father and mother.
My room was on the second floor to the left.

The house by the canal today.

A family photo with Seurn, myself, Wantha and Chittra
in front of photos of my parents, around 2005.

With some of the local villagers at Cha Huoy.

With the children at Mercy Home # 2, Kompong Chnang.

With one of my 'special' children from the Kampot project.

PART 3
MY THIRD LIFE

Picture taken just before publication: (from left, clockwise) Wantha, Thavy (Seurn's daughter), Seurn, me.

14

FINDING MY PLACE
(THE 1980'S)

As I started life again in Phnom Penh, I was a young woman with a new name and, like every other Cambodian, a heavy cloud of sadness and regret sitting over me. When I saw our old home it brought back memories of the family and the life we had lost. Staying there would have reminded me of this every day so Wantha and I had no interest in trying to reclaim it. Like our first life, it belonged to the past.

How to cope with such grief, anger and regret?

Amidst the wreckage of an entire society the new government decided to make medical training a priority. Wantha was already two years into a medical degree but initially she delayed returning to study medicine, as she needed to earn money for us to live. She got a job with the Ministry of Health as a bureaucrat dealing with the applications for training of nurses, medical assistants and midwives. This put her right at the centre of the government's plan to rebuild our medical system.

At that time in Phnom Penh, uncooked rice and jewelry were the main forms of currency. Public servants were paid in rice until a new paper currency was issued - the Cambodian riel. We were still a communist country and most of the new regime had been Khmer Rouge at some point. Their instincts were to have the government control everything, despite the fact that private trading was keeping people alive and goods flowing into and around the country.

I was now nearly twenty, had an education to grade 6, and was still naive about many things. I had no idea what I would do to earn a living or help my family and my country. One night, soon after returning to Phnom Penh, that changed.

I found out that our friends from Cha Huoy, Kosany and her mother Neak, were living not far from us in Phnom Penh. I asked Wantha to take me to visit them. Kosany had married a man called Ruos Samay, a cousin of Pen Sovan, the first Prime Minister after Pol Pot.

We went round for dinner to Neak's house one evening, but were scared to enter at first as these were now powerful people and we were just poor and displaced survivors and felt overawed. Neak was very glad to see us both and we shared a meal with them, which was both expensive and delicious.

After the meal Neak asked that I visit more often. She told her sons how I had brought her water for her bath at Cha Huoy, even though I had trouble walking or lifting. We talked a long time and Wantha told them what she was doing.

Then Neak asked a question that proved to be life changing for me.

"Laddha why are you not applying to study? Wantha works for the Ministry for Health. Why don't you? You can be a nurse or a medical assistant. You would be a good student."

"I don't know. I … I … can't apply because I … am related to Wantha. That is not allowed." This was true as working for the Ministry meant that a person's relatives were not allowed to apply and Sopheavy, Noem's daughter, had already been turned down because of it. I actually hadn't thought seriously about what I wanted to do, apart from picking up my education where I had left off.

"Would they let a disabled person do medical training anyway?" I asked.

"You should apply, Laddha. You are caring and hard working. Don't let them stop you. Maybe I can help you with this," Neak said.

Wantha also encouraged me but added that applications closed the next day. Neak asked her son-in-law, Ruos Samay, if there was anything he could do, as he was well connected with the nascent regime. Neak had made clear over the evening of her affection for me, and her gratitude for what I had done for her. She saw a chance to repay some of that kindness. Samay also wanted to show gratitude and contacted his colleague, Nou Beng, who was the Minister of Health, about the issue.

The Minister gave permission straight away for me to do medical training, noting that to do otherwise would be consigning me to being a beggar. However, even if I successfully completed the training, I still would not be allowed to work for the government due to my disability.

Despite this limitation I was surprised and thankful for how things had turned out. Over the coming years I stayed at Neak's house many times. She even asked me if I would like to come and live with her permanently. I thanked her but said I would not live separately from my sister any more.

The day after our visit, the sun was shining when my sister took me on her bicycle to the Nursing School to take the test. There were nearly 600 candidates for the 200 positions available, and I was the only candidate with a disability. To my pleasure, when the results came out I scored a 'two' and was told I would be studying to be a medical assistant to a doctor. I was on my way!

The medical assistant course would take three and a half years. Sopheavy (Noem's daughter, who had now changed her name to Marina) had also been allowed to take the exam and had passed too. She would be studying to be an assistant nurse.

The Nursing School had many students from the provinces and they had to be found accommodation. They stayed in apartments at the Nursing School, which were divided into two groups by gender. Students from the same province shared rooms with each other.

Students from Phnom Penh, like me, had to travel to the school from home. The Nursing School gave each student a scholarship of 45 riels per month. 30 riels were taken for our meals, leaving us 15 riels for study materials and anything else we needed.

My problem was how to get to the lecture hall every day. The school was about 5 kilometres from our apartment in Borey Keyla. The only transport was either by pushbike or cyclo and I could neither ride them nor afford to pay anyone for a lift.

In desperation, I said I would sleep on the verandahs of the school each night but Wantha would not allow me to live like that. We tried to get permission for me to stay in the student accommodation but this was against the rules as I wasn't from the provinces. Also there were already four students in each room and only two beds. Where would I stay?

I was nearly ready to give up when Marina came to my rescue. She had a friend from the Pol Pot regime days who was staying in the student accommodation and asked her if she would take me in. I said I would happily sleep on the floor and she and her roommates agreed.

This arrangement had to be kept secret from the monitoring teacher who would check on us all each night. I had to sneak into the room when it was getting dark. This turned out to be how I spent each night of my medical training!

These were strange times. Although it was an offence to study French for political reasons, the only textbooks for our course that had survived the war were in French. The lecturers used these books, translating the words into Khmer as they taught, as many students could not speak French anyway. We had to make our own notes on anatomy and biological systems as best we could.

Every day, 200 students squeezed into the lecture hall. There were no amplifiers or microphones so it was very difficult to hear what was being said. Fighting erupted every morning for places near the front before it was eventually decided that provincial students would sit on one side of the hall, and the Phnom Penh students on the other. I was often stuck at the back.

Everyone had to choose between midwifery and nursing: all except me, that is. I was told I would not be allowed to study midwifery.

When I asked about the reasons for this an official told me: "If you can't stand properly how could you expect to be a part of delivering babies?"

"If I can learn about this area I can do other things that don't need me to stand up," I countered. "I can study gynecology, I can help the mothers. You shouldn't stop me from doing this. I am a Cambodian woman so I should be allowed to study midwifery."

In truth I suspected that I would probably not have my own children but still wanted to have some connection to the birth process that all mothers go through. Despite the importance to me of studying midwifery and my protestations, the Nursing School just refused so I enrolled in nursing instead.

To my surprise I was the only woman enrolled in this particular nursing course, studying alongside over 100 males. Over the next three years I worked hard at my course, making friends from all over Cambodia and came to see myself as a health professional. I also came to be comfortable in the company of men.

In October 1983, on completion of the nursing course, there was great sadness that we would have to leave each other and go our separate ways. We had grown close. Everyone's story was different but all lost loved ones during Pol Pot's reign. Now at least we would have our opportunity to make life better for the survivors and their children.

I wanted to be part of that and play my role. What work would I get? Would I be allowed to work at all? How would I get to work? There were so many questions waiting to be answered. I was so worried about all this that I could not sleep well or eat much. We waited to see who would get work and where they would be sent.

Life was hard in those years for us. Our economy and infrastructure had been destroyed by the Khmer Rouge, who were still fighting from their jungle hideouts near the Thai border. The economy was dependent on our government, which did not approve of private trading, and western governments would not provide any investment so as not to appear to condone the Vietnamese invasion of Cambodia.

Wantha was the only one bringing in any regular money and so we never ate anything nice. Just prahok, pha-ak (both fish products)

and rice. There were now nine of us living in the apartment in Borey
Keyla. I desperately wanted to help but what could I do to earn
money? I took to studying out on the verandah, looking to the stars,
praying to the Buddha and waited impatiently for things to change.

AFTER several weeks, the announcement about our job locations
was made. All those who had applied for jobs were given a number
and numbers one to 20 would work at the Russian Hospital. My
sister told me I was number 20! I had a job!

My darkest fears had been of not having a job and being unable to
show what I **could** do. My two role models, Wantha and my mother,
had worked and been respected for their abilities and I was scared of
being overlooked because of my disability.

To get any job at that time was difficult. To be a woman and to
have a disability in our country made it even harder. My need to be
seen as useful by others had strengthened within me. I knew work
was the key to my fulfillment and now I had been given the chance.

The Russian Hospital was, and is still, the biggest in Cambodia,
with many departments. It was being rebuilt in 1982. At this time the
only assistance Cambodia received was from Vietnam and countries
allied to the Soviet Union. These latter countries sent us many doctors
and I started as an assistant and translator for them.

After working for short periods for a couple of doctors I was
asked to work as interpreter with a Russian doctor called Alexander
Safanos, who was a specialist in contagious diseases. The local Cambodians said he was a gruff, unpleasant, abrasive and intolerant man
and they didn't want to work with him. As a result they had given
him the nickname 'Tetanos' (as in the disease tetanus).

One day I was told I would be working with Dr. Safanos. I stood
there with my previous boss as he told the Russian about my person-
ality, my work ethic and what I was good at. Dr. Safanos looked me
up and down and I thought he would refuse to work with me, but
the next day we started our work together.

After a few days we seemed to warm to each other. I felt he was a
good doctor as he was kind to the Khmer patients. I found out that

the assistants Dr. Safanos had worked with before were often late to work and did not do a good job translating his questions into Khmer for the patients. He was not happy with their work.

Communication was always going to be a problem for Dr. Safanos. He spoke hardly any Khmer and few locals spoke Russian. I spoke a little Russian but wasn't assertive enough to suggest using my embryonic language skills, so we just muddled by.

After a little investigation, I discovered that the only Cambodians who spoke any Russian were some engineers, just back from training in the USSR. Unfortunately they had set the doctor up for ridicule by teaching him wrong translations into Khmer. When it came to the phrase "Good morning" they taught him the Khmer equivalent of "I love you". The Russian "Vitamin B complex" became the Khmer "Don't forget sweetheart". When the patient giggled or looked bemused, the poor doctor Safanos had no idea why. This joke of mistranslation also undermined him in the eyes of the Cambodian nurses, who thought him to be rude and arrogant.

I couldn't just sit back and allow this to continue so decided to sort out the engineers by letting them know that I knew what they had done. I also warned them I would tell the doctor what was going on unless they did something about the situation and that the hospital would refuse to see them if they were sick.

After that, when the engineers chatted to Dr. Safanos in Russian, they told him to change the phrases and taught him the correct ones, saying the people might understand the new phrases better. Dr. Safanos also found out that I spoke a little Russian when I corrected him over a translation from French. We got on increasingly well and he wanted me to stay working with him.

In 1986 the Russians started to leave Cambodia and Dr. Safanos was one of those who packed up to go. He said that I could come to Russia to have an operation to fix my leg. There were too many unknowns for me, however – snow, cold weather, and no one there who knew me apart from Dr. Safanos – so I didn't take him up on the kind offer.

His job was now to be done by a Cambodian female doctor,

called Reaksy. I stayed on and worked with her for a few months continuing as before, until one day I received a letter from the hospital.

It said that because of my disability I could no longer work in my current role or in any medical role at the hospital, and that I would be transferred to work at the Technical Office. There I would collect and process statistics for the hospital.

I felt totally crushed. I was good at my job, worked hard, and there had been no complaints about what I did. None of this mattered it seemed. As I had a disability my good record counted for nothing.

Inside, I raged against the injustice of this treatment, but kept my tears there, unwilling to show others how hurt I was. I knew I had no choice but to accept it and move on.

My new responsibilities were to track the statistics of inpatients and outpatients, keep files up to date, and report to the Ministry of Health. There were 17 inpatient sections and 23 polyclinic-consulting departments. At that time there were no computers and everything had to be written by hand or typewriter. I did all this work with a colleague in a side room just off the main office.

My disappointment with the situation motivated rather then depressed me. I decided that I was going to work harder at this job than I had ever worked before. If I got behind at work I would even come in some weekends. They would *never* again be able to use my physical weakness as an excuse to take away what was important to me.

I made up three mottos that would remind me about the person I wanted to be.

"Even if I am looked down upon, I will make myself be respected.
Even if I have little, I will use what I have to move ahead.
Even if I do not have much knowledge, I will give everything and become a skilled person"

These mottos drove me to success at work, constantly reminding me of the sort of person I had to be to succeed. I have continued to work at the Russian Hospital since that time. My colleagues and I never quarrel or accuse each other of anything. From the administrators to the doctors and the ladies I work next to in our office, we all get on so well.

The opportunity that was given to me by Neak's influence allowed me to become a competent, respected, professional in an important public institution. This gave me income, minimal though it has always been, and a place in the adult world of work. Without this foundation, this first step up the ladder, my other achievements could never have happened. For this I will always be grateful.

15

THE LIGHT GETS IN
(EARLY 1990'S)

THE 1980'S were a bleak time in Cambodia. Our society had been literally destroyed and no family was unaffected by this. Our best and brightest were dead and those left were traumatised. We who survived had to get on with living.

My life at this time was a fog, in which I stumbled, unfulfilled, but not knowing why. I was glad I had a job but it didn't bring me joy, or any hope that my life could rise to any great heights. I was demonized by spirits and dutifully fulfilled my obligations of sacrifice to the Buddha.

Gradually I decided to live my life essentially alone, and avoid the dangers of any dependency or disappointment. To make it tolerable I had my sister and the remnants of my extended family.

Towards the end of the decade the fog started to lift and I sensed opportunities that hadn't been there before. In 1987 the Vietnamese occupiers said they were leaving which probably meant the West was coming to our rescue. What would it all mean for me?

In 1990 King Sihanouk returned to Cambodia and everything began to change. The Vietnamese withdrew and the international community did decide to come and help us to become a more democratic and prosperous country. We saw blue military uniforms in

Phnom Penh, representing the United Nations (UNTAC – United Nations Transitional Authority in Cambodia), because the Khmer Rouge had not given up the fight and continued to cause trouble and violence in the north-west of the country.

Most importantly, sanctions were lifted so foreign investment started to flow into the country. With the funds came people and virtually none of them could speak Khmer. Very soon there were over 50 nationalities here and this was obviously going to be good news for anyone who could speak a foreign language. I could speak French, English, some Russian and some Thai and so expected to be in demand.

Interpreters would be very sought after. Salaries for such jobs started from $200 a month and went as high as $1,000 a month. My hospital salary in 1990 was about $5 - $10 a month.

I knew several people who started getting work as interpreters for hotels, non-government organisations (NGOs), restaurants or companies. Surely I would get a job as well and lift my quality of life. I kept my job at the hospital but went part time, only working mornings, so I would have time for other opportunities either in the afternoon or evening.

I wrote my *curriculum vitae* and posted it to several NGOs, and anywhere else that could be interested. However there soon appeared to be a pattern in the responses I was getting. They all seemed to tell me: "We are sorry but we only need those who are in good physical condition".

One example I remember particularly well was in 1992 when my niece, Daly, who could speak reasonable English, came by and asked for my help in trying to get a job. She was employed at the 'Kampuchea' newspaper but wanted to work using her language skills. We took our CVs to several NGOs and private companies but again it ended with "we could use your language ability but we are sorry we don't have a role for you."

This continued refusal to give me a chance to work at a job that I knew I could do gnawed at me. However, as is the Buddhist way, I did not let it show and on the surface remained calm. It finally came to a head when Daly and I went to a place called the Independence Guest House near the UNDP (United Nations Development Program) office.

We got there early in the morning before 8.00am and climbed to the second floor. We explained our business - we would do anything the job required, (even cleaning) if it needed English speakers - and handed in our CVs to the Khmer receptionist.

"Thank you Miss," she said. "Please sit over there and we will deal with you in good time." A few hours later Daly approached the secretary again.

"Is there anything else we have to do, Miss. We have been here since eight o'clock."

"Just wait and you will be seen by someone soon," she replied, without looking up from her typewriter.

We sat until nearly midday. The Cambodian male interviewers came out of their office and started to head for the door. They were going to just leave us waiting there! I found strength in my legs and pushed myself up between the men and the door. They looked at me, eyes wide, and stared. Words failed them for a moment but they didn't fail me.

"We have been waiting here all morning and we are still here. Are we going to get an interview for the jobs? My niece and myself speak good English and we want to work. Others have been here and left already."

"We only want to interview people who are in good physical condition," the older one said.

"Then why didn't you tell us this when we arrived?" I replied, wedging myself closer to him. "What about her", I said, pointing to Daly. "She is in good physical condition."

"She is too young," he responded. I knew what he meant to say was that she wasn't pretty enough for him.

"Then why did you allow us to wait and wait if you were never going to interview us?" I felt my face flushed red, and I shook a little, as my legs lost their strength. But I hadn't finished.

"Why did you make us waste our time here?", I fired at him. "Do you look down on us? Are we not worth any respect? Are we human or not?"

The older man's face changed. His eyes averted mine and his hand scratched the back of his head. He and his partner both looked at each other wondering what to do now. Although I had become self-conscious about my aberrant, confronting behaviour I still didn't move and waited, feeling the momentum was with me. It felt good.

"Okay, you can have an interview," he said. The job advert had said they needed English speakers, so he asked me a question in English, which I replied to appropriately. Daly and I followed him through to the office. After a brief interview he said he would contact us the next day, which of course he never did.

After a few of these type of incidents I felt very disheartened and stopped dreaming that I could get such a job. I gave up thinking about buying new clothes and decided to start writing my stories again to help survive. As a means of generating extra income I had become a writer of love stories. In the wake of the Pol Pot regime's destruction of all things cultural, there were no books available. From this, there had emerged a market for hand-written books that were hired-out from what was a library of sorts.

I had previously written two stories, based on tales that Mum had translated from Thai and read to me as a child. They had proved to be very popular, and earned me a little money. I used a pseudonym so no one would know it was me writing about such things!

However, sometime after the interview disappointments, my friend Pin Leaksmy, whom I had known since 1981, told me she had got a job with UNTAC and was now teaching foreigners to speak Khmer. One night she came round and asked me if I would be a substitute teacher for her students. Suddenly, just like that, I had a job with UNTAC and for the first time I could now call myself a language teacher – even if it was only as a substitute.

Several months later Leaksmy moved from UNTAC to an NGO called SAO (Southeast Asian Outreach - a Christian, British-based NGO). She knew a foreign student called Agnes Verner, who worked for SAO. Agnes was Canadian, with an Irish husband who was the director of the organisation in Cambodia, and they had worked in Thailand for more than 30 years.

One evening Leaksmy took me to meet Agnes at the office behind Wat Lungka pagoda. Leaksmy was leaving for a while and she introduced me as her temporary replacement.

Agnes wanted to learn Khmer and we spoke a few words in Thai to each other. I was so nervous that I could only say "kha, kha" ("yes, yes"). Despite this she asked me to come round and teach her at 4.00 pm the next day – 14 February 1993.

This was a very auspicious day as my brother Chittra also flew in from France to visit us. I was becoming hopeful about my life again.

Agnes learnt some words with me then gave me a red printed book with Khmer phonetics on one side and the English translation on the other. It was called "Modern Spoken Cambodian" and written by Franklin Huffman.

I couldn't read the Khmer side, as the phonetics used were an attempt to approximate Khmer sounds but derived from 'normal' alphabet letters. My native Khmer script has a completely different look and phonetic structure.

Luckily I could read the English translation and therefore work out what most of the symbols stood for in Khmer. My job was to translate the book into Khmer script. I was soon teaching as well as translating and my income quickly outstripped what I had been earning at the hospital.

In 1993 UNTAC needed to recruit local staff to work on running the election for a new Prime Minister and Leaksmy asked me if I wanted to be part of that. I got permission from Agnes and worked at the polling station at Wat Lungka pagoda for the three days of the election. I was so proud to be part of the political process of building a new, democratic Cambodia – and earned US$200 for the privilege!

One month later Leaksmy returned from what she had been doing and was ready to work again as a teacher at SAO. I knew this would mean I was no longer required and would have to leave SAO, finish writing the language textbooks and say goodbye to everyone.

I finished translating in my classroom downstairs and was

preparing my things to leave, only just holding back my tears. I had loved the organisation, the people and what I was doing. I had at last found something that I was good at, enjoyed and was of value to others. I didn't want to say goodbye.

Leaksmy came to me and apologized for taking my students from me, but it wasn't her fault. After all, she had got me this job and I was grateful for that. As I readied to leave, the SAO team emerged from a meeting on the first floor and I braced myself for the bad news. Agnes approached me and I looked down, trying to make it easier for her to tell me I was no longer required.

"Addheka, we want you to stay on as one of our teachers. We also need you to translate and write some textbooks for us."

I didn't know what to say and really had no idea they would keep me on. "Thank you", came to my lips, and I put my hands together and bowed a little.

Agnes and some of the others who were there smiled at me and said I was welcome. I then said goodbye to everyone, knowing that I was coming back the next day. I worked alongside the three permanent teachers, mainly writing the textbooks. It took me a year to translate the textbook by hand, an hour each day.

Gradually the number of students increased, as friends of Agnes and other foreigners came to study in Cambodia. We were even asked to recruit more Cambodians who could teach Khmer. Soon we had assembled a team of seven or eight teachers and even did some training at the Cambodian British Center.

Over the next three years, I became very close to Agnes. She trained Leaksmy and I to be better teachers and I came to know more about Christianity. I came to see her as my adopted mother.

Agnes, Leaksmy and I all worked together at the school and by June 1997, it was decided that the "Khmer School of Language" (KSL) would be handed over to its Cambodian staff. The question then was: who would take over as its leader?

Leaksmy had brought me into the organisation and was probably more experienced than me. There were also other teachers who had become part of the school. I was probably more shocked than anyone when Agnes asked me to be the principal of the school.

I had no idea that SAO had faith in my ability to lead the teachers and to deliver the curriculum. There was even a handing-over ceremony attended by embassy staff. It was a public affirmation of their confidence in me.

I was 36 years old and for the first time in my life had been given responsibility to make decisions that impacted the welfare of others. If I was not up to it, the school would fail, the staff would lose their job, and SAO's gift to Cambodia would be wasted. For me it was an awesome challenge and I would give it everything.

I took leave from the Russian Hospital for three years and spent all day at the school. Some teachers were unhappy with my appointment. They either didn't like me, or didn't want to be managed by a woman with a disability, so they left. Some of them used the KSL brand in setting up their own school. Those of us who remained struggled hard to keep the school going.

KSL was now a private school that had to survive on its own financially. Income had to be greater than expenses. There were two major expenses - teachers' wages and rent for the building. Some months there was very little salary and teachers had to find other jobs as well. For a while I did not take a salary and, in 2000, went back part-time to the hospital even though the salary was so little.

To try and create an adequate income for my teachers, I began a self-help scheme at KSL, which revolved around us developing a small-holding (small farm) together. However this meant them donating 10 per cent of their already meager wages to the scheme. I bought a plot of land - about half an acre - for $4,500 with my own savings and set about trying to earn money from it. The plot was about an hour from the city, in the Takhmao District of Kandal Province.

We tried raising pigs, growing morning glory, and even dug a large pond to produce fish. There were some successes along the way but it wasn't working out as we had planned. Pigs eat a lot, crops often all come ripe at the same time so prices are rarely good, and fish were hard to catch without draining the pond. It proved to be very difficult to make money.

By 2000 I had spent over $20,000 of my own money keeping KSL afloat and the rent was now US$800 a month. The stress of keeping the school going took its toll on my health and I became quite sick. This was not what I expected when I agreed to be School Principal.

With so much of our income going on rent, by 2004 the school was heading into bankruptcy. With each lesson around $5, it would take seven or eight lessons every day just to pay for the building rental.

Once again in my life Wantha came to the rescue. She had continued her medical studies and had worked as a doctor in the Ministry of Health since the early 1980's. We looked around for a building suitable for a language school and came across a row of brand new, three-storey buildings, near the Russian Markets. Wantha decided to buy the building for us and in so doing saved KSL from having to close its doors.

We have been there ever since. We have rooms for individual and group lessons and, as of 2015, employ around 13 teachers.

16

MY SPIRITUAL JOURNEY

I HAVE been a Christian since the early 1990's, but have always been someone who was trying to be in touch with God. My spiritual journey has been torturous and littered with dead ends and spiteful accusations. At one point I was so angry with my chosen gods and angels that I scolded them severely, then crouched in fear awaiting their wrath. It never came. What did happen was ... but I am getting ahead of the story.

Spiritual life in Cambodia has dominant influences from Buddhism (Theravada) and animism, which is a worship of animals or inanimate objects. They both shaped my views of myself and the world - especially the influence of my mother's Buddhist temperament and notions. The hallmarks of Cambodian Buddhism are tolerance, compassion and harmonious personal relationships.

Animism on the other hand reflects a more fearful view of the world. There are powerful forces for good and bad that must be placated or won over. Good spirits (angels) are to be encouraged and called on to help ward off evil spirits and ghosts.

There are other spirits as well, the best known being the *neak ta*. I saw the *neak ta dambouk* (spirit of the hill) when I was alone in Cha Huoy. Others told me what I had seen and it petrified me. I saw the '*Preah Inn*', and was demonized by the *mreng konveal*. Rathya was taken away by the spirit of *Khleang Meung*, despite Mum trying to appease it by freeing birds.

There are spirits that look after your house when you are away - *jumneang phteas* - and there is a particularly cruel spirit - *khon kror* - that can be assuaged and offer you serious protection, but whose payment involves killing (and roasting) of premature babies. As you can imagine it can become quite overwhelming if some people see themselves as being controlled by such evil influences.

The combination of the two influences, Buddhism and animism, suggests a life that is to be accepted gracefully, rather then struggled against, and one that must balance the good and evil spirits that are all around us. That is, in a nutshell, how I felt about my spiritual existence before 1993.

My spiritual beliefs are especially important to me because of my experience during the Pol Pot regime. As all supports were removed from my life – my father, my mother, my brothers, my home, my sister Wantha – I was forced to look within for comfort. I couldn't talk to anyone about my thoughts, feelings, or fears.

For the New People still living, they were suffering just as much, perhaps even more if, like Wantha and Prong, they had to work in the fields every day without rest. At least later, I had had the relative 'comfort' of being around the cooking hut and the village. For the Old People and the soldiers, such 'weakness' would inspire contempt and provide an excuse to get rid of a useless city girl.

When the rains fell and I was cold; when I almost drowned by falling into a pond and was barely saved; when my mother died of starvation in my arms, I could only appeal to the angels to listen to my plight. There was no one else.

Sometimes I felt they listened. After I saw the *neak ta damboung*, when Wantha had left me to return to the work camp, it was proof that these spirits existed, and could even play with me whenever they wanted. The angels were my only shield against such demons and I silently thanked them as I continued to see another day and another season.

As the country opened up following the departure of the Vietnamese soldiers, expectations about an improved life grew. The world we were being exposed to by the UN staffers was one of being able to earn money, a serious work ethic, and reward for effort.

All my ambitions became focused on being part of that world. The closer I got, the greater became the frustration when my hopes were dashed on the rocks of discrimination. My spiritual crisis came to a head the day I have previously described, when Daly and I went to the job interview and were ignored, in a way that left me traumatised and rudderless.

At the end of that day I arrived home totally washed-out. Again I had let my hopes lift me up before coming crashing down. I was thinking deeply about my life and why I was blocked from being who I wanted to be. I wanted to know why my prayers to the Buddha were not being answered. I looked up at the sky;

'If this world really has an angel that walks around this earth, and the gods are real, why do they play with my life like this?' I said to the Buddha.

'I give sacrifices (bananas) when it is your day Buddha. Half moon or full moon, I never forget even one. Why don't you help me get a job? Why do people look down on me? When I studied nursing, when I work at the hospital, people always look down on me. They only see what I can't do, not what I can.' My torment now took me somewhere new.

'From now on I will stop believing in you Lord Buddha. I will not worship you any more. If there is a God with the spirit that has the power to let them choose me to work, I will pray to it with a lot of fruit every day.'

After I had scolded the angels and the Buddha, I was afraid of what I had said and became scared. I thought they might be angry with me and destroy my life or have something bad happen to me.

Later that afternoon I fell asleep. I woke up suddenly and felt a presence in the room. I opened my eyes and saw a body and face with green skin. It looked like *"Preah Inn"*, a kind of demon, standing in the middle of my bed looking at me. I couldn't see the face clearly but I felt it was smiling at me.

I sat up in awe and fear. Then it disappeared and I moved outside as quickly as I could and saw the grandma who lived next door.

"I am so afraid," I told her. "I saw the '*preah inn*'. It had green skin and stood before me." She smiled and used this experience as a premonition to be used in the lottery that week. She won quite a bit of money and gave some to me as a reward!

As I reflect on my journey, this was a turning point. I had forsaken all the good spirits and the God Buddha and was now on my own. But I had nothing to replace them with. I was adrift.

It was at that time I came within the orbit of the SAO through Agnes and Jim Verner. The presence of Christian organisations in Cambodia was new. As part of the opening to the west, religious NGO's were officially allowed in Cambodia. My work with them as a translator and teacher of Khmer brought me into touch with their beliefs.

Inevitably I questioned the motives and actions of these people but found comfort and alignment in what they did. The Christian Bible was like blank sheets of paper though – it meant nothing to me. Although their beliefs seemed meaningless, I was simply happy to be working with friendly people in a job where my disability was irrelevant.

Over time we became much closer friends and, because of their evangelical nature, the Verners spent a lot of time with me and gave me a Christian narrative that started to resonate, ever deeper.

Agnes and Jim told me my life had a divine purpose, which was to help the poor people of Cambodia. They knew my story and said having a disability had been part of this plan. I had been spared from death in the Killing Fields of Cha Huoy, and had remained in Cambodia because God had this role for me.

Gradually what the Verners said made sense and it felt less like I had an empty space at the centre of my life. My Burmese friend MyPearl also helped me on this path.

I had been reluctant to go into church because, strange as it may seem, I thought you had to kneel to pray. I couldn't bear to have to be helped to get back up again and so avoided that ignominy by refusing to go in. Later, a near death experience in a *cyclo* accident that I was involved in with MyPearl, suggested to me that there were spiritual forces competing for my loyalty. I had to decide – was I with God or not?

That day after we had nearly been killed I felt different and finally went into a church. It was as if something new was happening to me. In the Anglican Church they were giving communion, where bread and wine is eaten as the symbol of the body and blood of Jesus. As I walked up to receive communion, the pastor, Don Cormack, said I could not yet take part as I didn't know God. I said I did know God, but he smiled and asked me to talk to him after the service.

Don brought me a book, the "Living Waters", which explains about becoming a Christian.

"Most people," he said, "need to study this for a year before they are ready to know God." Rather than a year, I was accepted within a month.

In June 1994 I was baptized as a Christian. This was not the end of my journey, but my life now had a strong direction and I had a powerful way to interpret the world and my place in it. Over the next few years I had many temptations and problems to overcome. I reflected a lot on my life and the meaning of what I had been through.

As I began to develop the Aid Projects of Mercy, which are described in the next chapter, problems arose, which to me, as an inexperienced and trusting language teacher, seemed insurmountable. However, since becoming a Christian and working hard to live by Christ's ethics, whenever I most needed help it has appeared, and this strengthened my faith.

In the nick of time, Wantha provided the money to buy the building for KSL, saving the project from bankruptcy; donors appeared just at the right time to allow my projects to continue; and, as will be told later, Thavy, *bong* Seurn's daughter, joined me and helped out her auntie by teaching poor widows to sew, staying involved as a leader and a devoted colleague.

Without these miracles my work would not have survived and what I see as God's plan for me would have come to nothing.

I RETURNED to Cha Huoy for the first time late in December 2014, stopping to pray in the car before we turned off the National Road # 5 and drove down the dusty, pot-holed track.

We first came to Ampil Choung, the village where we lost Ratana and Rathya, who lie with no grave to remember them. Looking around on both sides at the unending, treeless flat rice fields, I remembered being dumped there one night with my family 40 years ago.

I had had to think long and hard about why I was going back and what I would say to any of the *neak moulthan* if I could find them. Would I feel vengeful or be able to forgive them? Would they remember me? Would there be trouble with any of their descendants? Was Pet still alive? Could I maybe find Mum's resting place?

The first person I ran into was a young woman who was sitting inside a very small thatched building that was her shop. I told her something of why I was there but she couldn't help me. She hadn't been there that long she said. I felt uneasy, even scared, so decided against pushing further into the village and left shortly after, taking some pictures with my new acquaintance, whose name was Chran.

On a second visit, two months later, I took my friend Vanda along as security. He is a police detective who has been involved with our projects since the beginning. I wasn't sure how the locals might react to my being there, digging around and asking questions about the past.

Some parts of rural Cambodia are still quite wild and unpredictable, given the poverty and the enormous mental health legacy of the Pol Pot years. This unresolved trauma continues to blight the lives of survivors and those around them.

More people turned up at Chran's small shop this time to meet me, including some men around 30 years old. They were apprehensive and a little flustered. We chatted and laughed edgily. They knew why we were there but probably didn't know what to do about it. I decided to push things a little. I got out of the car and sat in my wheelchair amongst them. I bought fruit drinks from the icebox for everyone. I asked about Pet - was she still alive, where did she live? They knew who I was talking about but couldn't or wouldn't help me.

Their responses were all dead ends. "They may not be alive ... they don't live here now ... I don't know where they would be."

As I listened and watched their reactions to my questions, I knew the *neak moulthan*, and their children, were still scared. They knew what they had done was wrong and that if you killed someone's family, they would be angry with you and likely seek vengeance. So they still live in fear, still hide, still lead lives blighted by the past. I see this as God's judgment on them.

I have never had the opportunity or the impulse to take revenge. When we were back in Phnom Penh in 1981, the *neak moulthan* were not there. I tried to handle my grief and loss by feeling regretful, and telling myself what had happened was destiny. But it never worked for me, never really gave me a way to see myself as anything other than a victim.

Buddhism teaches us to bury our emotions, and talk the words of forgiveness. But Christians give bad things that have happened to them in the past to God. He is a judge and delivers justice in his own way. When you open your heart to God, you free yourself from having to take responsibility for that. And so you have the energy and resolve to do good things that help people who need it today. That is what my life has been about since I became a Christian.

17

AID PROJECTS OF MERCY (2000 TO THE PRESENT)

ONE DAY in 1999, my friend Leaksmy brought a young girl to the KSL. Her name was Dany and she was from Prey Veng province, close to Phnom Penh. She was a very attractive girl with long black hair sometimes tied up in a bun.

Her family was poor and, with Dany turning 16 years old, it was arranged that her uncle would employ her as a nanny for his children. He lived a long way from Prey Veng, in Poipet, close to the Thailand border. Unfortunately the uncle turned out to be a very depraved man. After he took Dany to his home he raped her and was planning to sell her to someone in Thailand, where she may have ended up in the brothels of Bangkok.

Dany ran away to escape from her uncle and came to Phnom Penh. A relative of Leaksmy saw Dany working in a restaurant advertising beer and brought Dany to Leaksmy. Dany did not want to do this any more as she was terrified about being found by her uncle, who she knew was looking for her. Leaksmy asked me if Dany could work at KSL as a cleaner and I agreed.

Dany had only grade three or four education and was not an academic child. She was happy to clean, earn enough money to send some back to her family, and feel safe from her uncle.

The arrangement worked well, but three months later, the uncle found out where Dany was working. He turned up at KSL and said I had no legal right to keep her, whereas he was her uncle, did have that right and was going to take her back to Poipet. I consulted a Human Rights lawyer and decided the best strategy was to adopt Dany as my daughter.

I brought her round to meet Wantha who was not convinced it was a good idea. She said she didn't like the way Dany always looked at herself in the mirror. Despite Wantha's advice, I announced to everyone at KSL that Dany was going to be my adopted daughter, and if anyone wanted to see her they had to go through me first. It was a bluff but it worked and we didn't see the uncle again.

The name Dany has an unfortunate association in a well-known Khmer drama. It suggests a girl who is always crying, hurt, separated from her husband, and attracting bad luck. Because of this I suggested Dany change her name to Meta, which means Mercy. She liked the name and so became Meta.

For a single girl as pretty as Dany/Meta, dangers lurk everywhere in Phnom Penh. We warned her to be careful but around the Water Festival time in 1999, she disappeared, as did another woman, Chariya, who had befriended Meta. We heard nothing for a month.

Then, one day, Meta turned up outside my house on a brand new motorbike, wearing expensive rings and a necklace. She knelt down before me and cried and told me what had happened. It is a very typical story of pretty young women in Cambodia.

Chariya had asked her if she would sleep with a VIP if she was paid $700. Meta's brother wanted money to buy two cows, and her mother wanted some material to weave some kramas. Meta said 'I am not a virgin because of being raped. I am earning only $70 a month in KSL.'

So Meta agreed and met with the man and slept with him. The arrangement lasted for a while, giving Meta temporary security, and money. She was treated well but, over the coming weeks, was passed along a chain of four people, ending up with a very well connected, rich Cambodian who put her up in a flat in Phnom Penh.

This man was kind to her but had a bodyguard who monitored whatever Meta did. He finally offered her the option to go back to her family in Prey Veng but she was still afraid of the uncle and was telling her family she still worked at KSL.

After the visit on the motorbike, I lost touch with Meta but recently one of the KSL staff saw her. They said Meta looked very thin – HIV thin.

After this experience, I wanted to do something to help the Dany's of Cambodia - and so did others. Two of these people were Robert Stirvey, a pastor from England, and his son Daniel. Daniel had been disabled by a car accident in England and had received significant financial compensation. Both father and son wanted to use that money to make a difference in Cambodia and had got in touch with Agnes, who led them to me.

The Verners, the Stirvey's, my friend Leaksmy and I discussed what we could do to make an impact on this issue. We talked about paying families money to prevent them from losing their daughters to traffickers or brothels. Maybe we could set up an orphanage? Most of our ideas fell apart when we thought them through, but our eventual conclusion was that there were two ways we could actually make a difference.

Firstly, in the short term, we should help very poor families to generate an income so they wouldn't be forced into selling their children - helping them to help themselves.

Secondly, in the longer term, we believed the answer was education. It is an almost impossible task for very poor families to prioritise education for their children when it costs money they don't have. For older youth, it is even harder to stay at school when they have to forgo opportunities to earn money. However, the usual prospect for families without educated children was being stuck in the cycle of poverty.

We decided to call our new venture "Aid Projects of Mercy", in memory of Dany/Meta. Our mission - that "God will bless the poor of Cambodia".

Where to begin? We knew we had to base our activities where

poor people lived, but close enough to Phnom Penh to allow us to be involved intimately with the project. We decided to start in a village called Prek Ho, in the Takhmao district of Kandal Province – less than an hour from the city.

The self-help farming scheme in Prek Ho that I had set up for KSL staff was not going well, so we decided that the associated plot of land could be the base. It was agreed the Stirveys would buy the land from me, and our project would have a home. I received $500 more from the Stirvey's than I had paid for the land, so this was shared with all my staff who had contributed to the self-help scheme.

Aid Projects of Mercy needed someone to be around full time and be our first 'field worker'. Mr Yin Ith, a tall, smiling, gentle man in his mid sixties who lived close by and had the time to volunteer became the anchor of the project.

I then used my funds to buy a wooden house for about $400 and erect it on the Prek Ho block. There we would train widows and poor girls to sew as a means of income generation. I bought five sewing machines, and got one of my nieces, Thavy (the first daughter of *bong* Seurn in his post Pol Pot family) to train the trainees, either on three-month or six-month courses.

We had ten students in the morning and ten in the afternoon. Some of the widows and poor girls subsequently used this training to secure jobs in the many clothing factories springing up all around Phnom Penh.

I also decided to use my funds to try and break the poverty cycle for a few, very poor families. We would give each of three families, 15 kg of rice and 50,000 riels (about US$13) a month for three months, hoping this would be enough to get them started on the path to self-sufficiency.

We also tried microfinance lending (putting up $100 for loans) and allowing a very poor family to live on the site. These first efforts had mixed results and we tried to learn from our mistakes and not repeat them.

Soon after this we moved onto the second part of our plan – how could we help ensure children in very poor families had the chance to go to school and attend it regularly? It was decided that we would provide writing books, pens and school uniforms for children who would be part of our project. But our funds were very limited compared to the large number of needy families. How could we decide who would receive our school materials?

The process we developed, which has been used subsequently on other sites, is to gather together a group of very poor children and their families, based on research from the area carried out by our team. I talk to everyone and publically confirm that the candidates for inclusion are indeed very poor and in need of help.

They must be serious at the government school, attend regularly, and look after what they are given. Both parents and children are told that I will know if they do not attend or are lazy at school. If this happens, they cannot stay in the project. Everyone knows what is expected.

We had now established something that began to impact upon the lives of a few very poor families. Their lives now had a positive momentum and they had more hope for their future. When friends and family members saw what we had begun in Prek Ho, they wanted us to help other poor people that they knew, and work in their area.

Over the next few years we developed a template for each of our Mercy Home projects. Each project has a base, either in a building we erected or in the home of a relative, big enough for 30 or 40 students to come together every day to learn, keep in touch or just play. It is a 'home away from home'.

Each project has someone who can teach literacy or maths and English. All students go to normal government schools, but we supplement their education costs to increase the chance they will succeed. Each year, in September, just before the school year starts, we give our children materials for school. We also teach the children to sing Christian songs. Our project now has 'homes' in 7 provinces. I spend most weekends being driven around the country by Thavy or Vanda, visiting our children and helping them with problems in their lives. I will do this as long as I am able.

EPILOGUE

Each year Wantha, *bong* Seurn, his daughter Thavy, Chittra (if he is in Cambodia) and I return to Touk Meas. We go to the pagoda at the end of the road that used to be home to our paternal grandparents - Seng Long and his wife, Kim Eva. We arrange with the monks to make offerings to the spirits of our ancestors while we are there. This ceremony is pictured below.

We remember our grandparents, who lived out their time as would reasonably be expected. We also remember our parents and our siblings whose life ended so abruptly, so unnecessarily and so tragically over a six month period in 1975 and early 1976. We remember them all;

Seng Long - Kim Eva - Seng Bou - Pan SutChay - Seng Sut Vanna - Seng Sut Phalla (Prong) - Seng Boun Ratana - Seng Boun Nora - Seng Boun Rathya.

Seurn and Thavy at the ceremony in the Touk Meas pagoda.

ACKNOWLEDGEMENTS

Addheka

I have been able to write this book of my life where others have not because of my determination to share my story. My courage for this comes from several places.

Firstly, from my parents, and the love they gave me while they could. They spent much time and money trying to overcome my disability and give their youngest daughter a life. I was 13 years old before this perseverance reaped its reward and I was able to walk. I hope they are proud of what their youngest daughter has achieved.

My second sister Wantha has been by my side my whole life. She has always been there for me with her encouragement, her love, her wisdom, and her resources. Her strength and courage in the face of adversity has always shown me the person I could be.

God saved my life many times during the Pol Pot regime, in order that I could be his disciple and help the poor of Cambodia. It is thanks to God that I am alive and able to serve his people.

My cousin Seurn, who carried me on his shoulders into the acupuncture room, has been a constant companion through my life and has been tested like all of us. His daughter Thavy continues that help by driving me around the country, being my personal assistant and being a leader in the Mercy Home projects.

I would like to thank Agnes and Jim Verner, without whom I would not have become a teacher and missionary. Finally I would like to thank Jim Pollock for his work in putting this book together. We worked well together for 18 months and made a great team.

Addheka
December 2015

Jim

The book was framed in large part by Addheka's memories and recollections. She was hardly a teenager when many of the heartbreaking events took place. Wantha's help in adding detail and context has greatly improved the narrative and allowed the depth of Addheka's experiences to be told more fully. Seurn also contributed his (fading) memories of the times. For both it meant revisiting emotions and memories they would rather leave alone. I thank them for their invaluable contributions.

I would like to thank Addheka for choosing me to be part of this worthy and inspiring project. To be touched by the lives of such people as Addheka and Wantha is to be truly blessed.

I would also like to thank my friends who helped bring the book to fruition. Without their support, both moral and editorial, it would have been a much harder road. Thanks especially to Steve Ireland for his skillful, laborious and thoughtful editing of the manuscript. Also to Judy Jackson and Corinne Gurry for their unfailing optimism and quality contributions to this project.

Finally I would like to thank my wife Elaine for her encouragement in allowing me to pursue such an uplifting endeavour. I have learnt that writing a book can be a lonely affair. Without the understanding of loved ones they would never be written.

Jim
December 2015.

APPENDIX 1: CHILDREN OF SENG BOU *

1. With Pan Sutchay *

1. * Vanna (female, born 1950)
2. Wantha (female, 1952)
3. Phalla (female, 1954, died after two weeks)
4. * Ratana (male, 1956)
5. Chittra (male, 1958)
6. * Nora (male, 1959)
7. Laddha (female, 1961), later Addheka
8. * Rathya (male, 1963)

2. With Lux Noem

1. * Nareth (Male, born 1960)
2. * Sokuntheary (female, 1962)
3. * Sideth (female, 1964)
4. * Sonasy (male, 1966)
5. Sopheavy (female, 1968), later Marina
6. * Sopheth (male, 1973)

3. With Prom Seylo

1. * SeylakVatei (female, born 1962)
2. * Sochupadey (male, 1964)
3. * Soktassei (male, 1966)
4. * Naradei (male, 1969)
5. * Noraingsei (female, 1970)
6. SeylakSakvaney (female, 1973)
7. SeylakKessaney (female, 1976)

* indicates that they died during the Pol Pot regime

APPENDIX 2:
CAMBODIA, A BRIEF HISTORY

French rule up to 1953

France was the undisputed colonial power in the region from around the 1860's until World War 2 and ruled Cambodia as part of French Indochina (Cambodia, Laos and Vietnam). When the Japanese swept through SE Asia, they tolerated the Vichy (pro Nazi) French until 1945. After that they pillaged the region, taking all the food they could steal in order to feed their own army. In 1941 the Japanese forced France to hand over Battambang and other Cambodian provinces to Thailand. These were returned in 1946.

Independent Cambodia; 1953 - 1970

In 1953 Cambodia was grudgingly granted independence by France and became the Kingdom of Cambodia under Prince Norodom Sihanouk. In neighbouring Vietnam the French continued to resist this, stating they did not want the country to become communist. They were finally defeated in 1954 at the battle of Dien Bien Phu, and left Indochina permanently.

Vietnam was then divided, North Vietnam under the communist regime of Ho Chi Minh, and South Vietnam under a succession of pro-western regimes. The North continued to agitate to unite the nation and this drew in the USA, in support of the anti-communist South. The military confrontation between the USA and its S

Vietnam allies on the one hand, and the communist forces under the banner of the National Liberation Front (NLF) on the other spilled over into Cambodia.

The NLF received supplies through the Cambodian port of Kampong Som (Sihanoukville), and from along the "Ho Chi Minh trail", which ran, in part, through Cambodia. Their soldiers also crossed the border from Vietnam to hide and shelter from the Americans. In 1969 the US started secret bombing all of the above regions inside Cambodia and this spread to the whole country and continued until 1973. The bombing destroyed much of Cambodian rural life and forced many people to choose between continuing to live in their village, and risk further bombing, or fleeing to urban areas.

Civil War; 1970 – April 1975

In March 1970, a clique of military and political figures led by Lon Nol ousted Prince Sihanouk by military coup. The monarchy was abolished and the country was renamed the Khmer Republic. The government of Cambodia now allied itself with the anti-communist forces in South Vietnam, and invited the Americans to come and destroy whatever communist forces they could find, Vietnamese or Cambodian. This polarised the country. The choice was now between an increasingly corrupt and bankrupt government, which supported the bombing, or joining the resistance, which fought under the banner of the still popular Prince Sihanouk.

Many villagers chose to fight for the inclusive resistance movement (the *maquis*) but this gradually became dominated by the 'red Khmers', better known as the Khmer Rouge. They were the best organised, receiving considerable support from China and Vietnam.

By 1973 the Khmer Rouge were mostly independent of Vietnamese support. Until 1975 the Khmer Rouge administered most of the country, with Lon Nol's forces pushed back into a few urban areas, mainly the capital Phnom Penh. The Khmer Rouge administered the 'liberated' areas and developed their increasingly intolerant and violent form of rule. They closed in on the capital and, on 17 April 1975, took total control of the whole country. In Vietnam, communist forces also marched into Saigon a few weeks later.

Pol Pot regime; April 1975 – December 1978

The new government declared their intention to rebuild "Democratic Kampuchea" from the start – "Ground Zero". Urban dwellers were sent to the country to work under the peasants, the "Old People", and the Khmer Rouge soldiers. All currency was destroyed and all private property except clothes and a few possessions were declared to belong to "*Angkar*" (meaning 'the organisation').

Anyone found out to have played a role in the Lon Nol regime was executed immediately. Over the next three and a half years the increasingly brutal dictatorship deliberately sought to destroy all remnants of the old society, including intellectuals, teachers, monks, students, professional people. This was done through execution, starvation and deliberate neglect. The paranoid Pol Pot regime saw enemies everywhere, and started to kill its own cadres. Some, in the Eastern Zone, saw this coming and fled over the border to Vietnam. After Pol Pot had needlessly attacked Vietnamese villages, the 'giant from the east' invaded Cambodia in December 1978. The regime collapsed in a few weeks and any surviving Khmer Rouge leaders fled westwards, to the Thailand border. One of the most brutal and violent regimes of the twentieth century was defeated. More than a third of the population had perished, including most of the 'New People'.

The Vietnamese 'occupation'; 1979 to 1993

The Vietnamese established the People's Republic of Kampuchea in 1979. For most of the next 10 years Vietnam occupied Cambodia, ensuring the Khmer Rouge did not return. They exploited the country's resources, especially timber, and ensured that the government they would eventually leave behind would be pro Vietnamese.

The tragedy of the Khmer Rouge period was now compounded

by the attitude of western powers. They did not want to help re-
construct the country, as this would appear to condone what they
considered to be an invasion (by the Vietnamese). As a result aid
was restricted to refugee camps near the Thai border and the population of Cambodia continued to suffer from the effects of a broken
economy and society.

The modern era; from 1993 to the present

Under the Paris Peace Accords in 1991, Vietnam pulled out of
Cambodia. The United Nations Transitional Authority in Cambodia
(UNTAC) was established to restore order and prepare the country
for free and fair elections. In 1993 the Royal Cambodian Government was established under coalition rule. Since then Cambodia has
been gradually opened up to the world and has set about rebuilding
a society that has lived through over 30 years of civil war and unprec-
edented violence.

APPENDIX 3:
STORIES FROM THE PROJECTS

The following stories are from my work with the poor of Cambodia over the last 15 or so years. The stories show how the poor of Cambodia eke out a living in the face of poverty that is the legacy of the Pol Pot years.

Fixing eyes and breaking legs

MADAM AGNES, whom I consider to be a mother and mentor to me, told me of a Doctor Ogden from America. He is an ophthalmologist who raises money in the US to fund trips to poor countries where he tests eyesight and provides glasses where required. Agnes told him about our projects and he agreed to visit each of our communities to test eyesight for anyone that needed it.

Working in the health ministry gave me an insider's view of how to best frame what we wanted to do to minimize bureaucratic holdups or having to pay bribes. The team was essentially donating their skills and materials, and referring any surgical cases, particularly for those older villagers with cataracts, to the appropriate medical centre. They would also provide some medication for conjunctivitis if required.

In 2007 we travelled for a week around 5 of our provinces, using our facilities as the base to test those who turned up. I had to organise the buses and accommodation and we moved south through Kandal,

Takeo, Sihanoukville, Koh Kong and Kampot. I would register those who asked for testing and they would be seen by one of the team of medical professionals. We would process about 60 people a day.

From our project in Saang district (Kandal province) we sent 18 older people to have the cataract operation in Battambang. APM (Aid Projects of Mercy) paid for their operations and for their transport and accommodation while they were there. This first visit was a great success and we arranged to visit our northern provinces on the next trip, two years later. This was not so uneventful for me.

During the Pol Pot regime, with so little food or energy, I walked with the use of a stick or crutch or whatever I could find. I didn't want to draw attention to my disability and tried to blend in. When I arrived back I was able to walk unaided until I put on some weight in the late 1990's. From then I needed a stick again.

In 2009, Dr. Ogden's team returned and we headed north for Battambang and Kampong Chnang provinces. When we arrived in Siem Reap on our bus, I agreed to continue into town to assist some of our medical experts do some shopping. The bus had quite a high step and I had descended from the bus before. On this occasion, however, I slipped while coming down and fell, most of my weight pushing down on the outside of my right leg, near my ankle. I heard a crack, and I felt a stab of pain. I had broken my leg.

I rang Wantha and she drove from Phnom Penh to pick me up (a 6 - 8 hour trip one way). Back in Phnom Penh an x-ray revealed a fracture just above my ankle. It had cracked in such a way that any pressure on the leg would force the fracture apart again.

The doctors said I would have to lie down for about 45 days while it healed. I made arrangements, with my cousin, Yaem's grand-daughter, who also worked at KSL, for her to manage the school while I was unavailable. After 45 days, another x-ray showed it would be another month, then another and another.

I had to lie down for a full year – as I had to do when I was 2 years old - to allow the fracture to heal. It was at this time I started to write down these memoirs. When I was allowed to get up I decided to use a wheelchair all the time, as I was scared of breaking my leg again and having to spend another year lying down. I can stand for a few minutes, and try to every day, but I never walk now.

Resisting the gangsters

IN PREK Ho village, the site of our first project, we met Yat when he was about grade 4. He was the oldest of 4 children, and his step-father was an amputee. The only income the family earned was by his mother selling honey, which she had trouble selling locally. We bought Yat a bicycle so he could get to school more easily – it was a long walk – but his mother sold it to get rice for the family.

Yat nearly gave up school many times, once even allowing a younger sibling to go in his place. Gangsters from the local area traffic women and children and sell drugs, making money from the misery of the poor. Yat was invited to join such a group and he considered it, just to be able to bring some money into the family.

We knew this was happening and tried to help him make a good choice. We continued to help his family by giving them rice each month and paying his school fees. This allowed him to come to the project in the afternoon, improving his English, literacy and numeracy. He resisted the gangsters approach, and finally graduated from high school.

At KSL we offer promising students like Yat the chance to go to university if they want. I have arrangements with the Western University in Phnom Penh, for a 30% discount on their fees, which APM pay. KSL gives them the chance to earn money while studying by teaching Khmer to foreigners. I train them how to teach and they find out if they have what it takes to be an effective teacher.

Yat was studying in his first semester when he fell in love with a young woman and they planned to marry. Her parents needed help on their small rice farm and Yat was going to work there, while his wife worked in a nearby factory. I told him to think long term about being a teacher or a farmer. He chose to stay and works with us at KSL today.

Fish and rods

AT PREK Ho, Mercy Home # 1, we constructed a small shelter and had a little land to grow vegetables. We came across a father called Muon Kea. He had two children, was homeless and literally eating off the streets of Prek Ho. He gladly accepted our offer to have a simple dwelling for his family and a chance to earn money. He grew broccoli, morning glory and some other vegetables, which he sold, helping him to purchase a *romoh* - a bicycle that can transport goods. He moved on with his life.

Students then told us about a woman who appeared to be homeless and in danger of starving. Her name was Neth. It turned out she was running away from a husband who drank too much and was violent towards her, and their three children. She lived a few kilometres from the project on the other side of a river that can only be crossed by ferry. We agreed to let her live in the small hut and to allow the project to be her base for a while.

To everyone's disappointment the husband found her, but appeared humble in accepting responsibility for his faults. His children were missing him and he begged to be allowed to stay. There was a range of opinion in our team. Should we let him stay or not? I said we should if Neth wanted to. He signed a contract that if the arguing and fighting continued he would have to go. One month later he was back to his old ways so, backed up by local police, we made him leave.

Neth stayed with us for a few more months, before returning to support her sick mother. By then she was pregnant again, and her children had dengue fever. This experience taught us that we have to know the limits to what we can do if we are to survive and remain available for the people in all our projects. Sometimes we have to help poor families with the next meal but if that is all, how will things ever change? How do we give them the fishing rod rather than just the fish?

One answer to that question emerged recently with an Australian supporter, who learnt Khmer with us. He wanted to help a family with 6 children he came to know. He is a very generous man and he bought a tuk-tuk for the father hoping to break the cycle of poverty for the family. Unfortunately with sickness the father sold the tuk-tuk and soon they were back to where they started.

We came up with an idea and held a meeting at KSL with our Australian donor, the whole family and me. The plan, drawn up with signatures and thumbprints, was for the 4 oldest children to come to the KSL on Friday after school, and stay the night there. They would be supervised and fed by our live-in teachers. The next day, from 8 in the morning until 4 in the afternoon, all four children would learn to read, speak and write English, after which they would go home.

Learning to speak English is a huge advantage for anyone in Cambodia. The opportunities to interact meaningfully with wealthy, friendly, foreigners can often translate into income, through tips, or gifts and many jobs in hospitality, tourism and other areas have English speaking as compulsory.

I ring up from wherever I am in Cambodia on Saturday and talk to them making sure they are working hard. This is working well and hopefully the children, the future of the family, will gain enough in education and English fluency to get to the first step on the ladder out of poverty.

Babies in very poor families

IN 2001 I went with my friend Leaksmy to visit her cousin in Kampong Thom. A woman approached us as we were having lunch and asked us if we could set up a project nearby in a very poor community. She had heard what we did. I had hardly begun Mercy Home # 1 and was in no position to help. I apologized but said it was not possible. Then she asked if I could take care of her baby, which she was having trouble looking after. Again I said I couldn't.

Some weeks later this lady turned up in our KSL office at Phnom Penh. It turned out she had been hiring out her baby son to a disabled beggar for 500 riels (12 cents) a day. They now wanted to buy the baby from her. He had been fed two small bananas a day and his health was now clearly perilous. His skin was covered in sores, he smelt badly and he probably had pneumonia as he couldn't breath easily. It was four o'clock in the afternoon and the mother had just left him there and taken off back to Kampong Thom. He was probably close to death and I had to decide what to do.

I still remember his little eyes looking at me as I thought what to do. I told the teachers to clean him in warm water, and give him some porridge. Then I rang Marina (Noem's daughter), who is a midwife and knew more about what to do next. She also has a kind heart like me.

She said to take him to the Kanta Bopha Children's hospital (set up by Dr. Beat Richner in 1992). He was going to be in there for a while so we hired a lady to look after him and feed him while he was there. I also gave him a name – Johan. Mothers in Cambodia often hold off naming their baby until it is over a year old in case it dies.

A week later Johan was recovering well when he and his minder disappeared from the hospital. We couldn't find either of them. We went to the hospital and asked what had happened. One nurse said he died but another said he had been taken by an "organisation". There was no paperwork to reflect this – he was just gone. The second nurse pointed to other examples of babies who had also just disappeared. They knew that Johan was not Marina's baby so that information almost certainly influenced what happened from there.

As I became more curious about this I learnt that many mothers dropped their children off at the hospital and left, when they could not care of it any more. What could the hospital do? When 'organisations' take them away it solves a problem for the hospital, and, it seemed to me, not too many questions were asked.

I believe Johan is alive and know that I had a hand in saving his life. Where he is now however, I have no idea.

A similar story had a different ending for Marina. As a midwife in Cambodia, mothers regularly ask midwives to look after their newborn babies. One mother who had her baby delivered by Marina got her phone number and rang her, saying she was going to throw her baby boy in the river if Marina didn't come and look after it.

Marina went to the mother and agreed to take it. The baby had already been put in the basket to be thrown into the river.

She said she would take the boy to an orphanage and have him tested for HIV. Marina took the baby home however, and Noem, Marina's mother, quickly fell in love with him. We all suggested a name, but Marina decided on Navid. Her 3 children grew to love Navid as well and he became a much-loved, spoilt member of the family. A happier ending!

The flower sellers of Tonle Bati

TONLE BATI, in Takeo province, has the ruins of a temple that attracts tourists to the area. I visited there with a student in 2003 and sat having lunch. We were soon bombarded with requests for money from child beggars. There were so many I felt I had to do something for them.

The children, and adults who hover around close by, live here and every day hope to cajole, harass, or smile their way to receive some riels from the tourists who come to visit. It is usually the girls who do this, some of them learning enough English to provoke a conversation.

I have been coming here now for over 10 years so have learnt a little about the community. Most are landless, their rice fields sold to buy food or cure poor health. Every time I come I meet two men who have a mental illness – perhaps the most pervasive form of disability in Cambodia. One is a short, loud, seemingly aggressive man who has a big belly and has never worn a shirt in all the time I have known him. Every time I say 'why do you never wear a shirt' he just looks at me. He frolics with the flower sellers quite roughly, but they don't seem to mind. The other is quieter, about 50, having just a few, isolated teeth that protrude with his big smile. He has a wispy beard and loves to chatter when I am there.

These men are often ridiculed and marginalized by their communities, probably unemployable, and try and somehow gather enough to survive. The flower sellers don't mind them and I usually give them both some money when I am there. The shirtless man looks after a sick mother, so I give some money for her, for which he is always grateful.

We decided in 2003 to set up a project here and give the school children our usual support; one pen and a notebook at the start of each school year. We thought we had funds for 30 children but had to push this out to 50 as there were so many.

We were thinking about which group we should focus on. 'Children' from grade 1 – 6, or 'youth' from grade 7 – 12. We found that youth rarely complete school because the need for them to work is so pressing, so they would be our focus.

Tonle Bati is close enough to Phnom Penh for youth and adults to be drawn into the work force, some from as young as 15, though this is against the law. There are hundreds of factories around Phnom Penh, some that employ over 1,000 women, making clothes or shoes for an international market. Now, in 2015, there is a building boom in Phnom Penh as foreign, mainly Chinese, investment flows into the country.

Males are in demand as labourers on construction sites, as guards or even parking attendants (who rely totally on tips). Labourers can earn between $3 and $5 a day, or between $70 and $100 a month. They often sleep on site, in hammocks strung up over the rubble and concrete.

Girls in clothing and shoe factories are currently fighting to raise their salary to over $120 a month. To put this in a wider Cambodian context, the girls will often not go home, but share a room with 4 or 5 others and pay around $30 a month just to live, including water and electricity. This leaves less than $2 a day to buy food and anything else they may need. There is no money left to be sent home and if there is sickness, they have nothing to cover this cost.

They can earn more money by working extra shifts (they already work a 48 hour week) but this then means they cannot return home to be with their parents, or be available to help out on the farm. As a result many farmers have to sell their land, and are then in danger of having no income.

The chance to earn money will ensure a flow of labour to meet the demand. APM try and offer a different option. If a youth can stay at school – at Tonle Bati we have several girls in our program – we offer them the chance to attend a Youth Camp, which we hold every year in Kampong Som (Sihanoukville). Here we train our volunteer youth to be Christian leaders in their communities. They learn about Jesus, Christianity and can choose to be baptized if they wish. They form the backbone of our projects.

Kunthea, my adopted son

Two hours north of Phnom Penh on National Road # 5, the road comes within a dozen kilometres of the Tonle Sap river at a village called Srah Keo in Boribo District of Kompong Chnang Province. Large tracts of the land between the road and the river were being bought up by the Tiger Beer Company, which means being lost to the local villagers and probably to rice growing. A friend of Wantha, a doctor from Pursat, wanted to reverse this trend by setting up a 'Green project" which would keep the land available for villagers. They wanted to know whether I was interested in buying some land for our projects?

At the time I wanted to try and grow our own rice so we could give it to poor families or sell it. In 2006 I agreed to buy 10 hectares, encouraged by funds from a donor from Agnes's network and a good price – only $150 a hectare. In my naïve enthusiasm I hadn't considered how we were actually going to farm it.

A farmer, Mr Roth, agreed to look after the land for the Pursat doctor and we got to know him. We went to his home, and were offered cakes cooked by his wife, and mother of their 4 children. One of them kept looking at me, and actually called me 'mak' (mother). His mum said I was 'neak kruu' (teacher) but he persisted. Over the next few visits I became very fond of this little boy, called Kunthea.

Utilising local knowledge we planted our first crop of rice in the 10 hectares. We learnt that both transplanting seedlings and harvesting is very labour intensive. Preparing the land, with a motorized small tractor, is expensive, and you also need somewhere to store the rice you harvest. Our team from KSL were involved in all of this, and at harvest time we spent several days there.

The second year things got harder still. We found we were competing against other farms for the labour to harvest the rice, and when this came too late, we lost some of the rice on the ground as it fell over. Once again I was becoming stressed by trying to make decisions about matters of which I had little knowledge or experience.

After two harvests we decided we had to do things smarter. We decided to rent out the land to local farmers and charge them a rent of 500kg of rice for each hectare they signed up for. We would also ensure they had rice seed, as this often got eaten or sold before seeding time. Also by providing the seed at that time, it was half the price of other times of the year.

I used some of my donated money to erect a concrete building on a block of land closer to the main road. This would be the hub of 'Mercy Home # 2'. Kunthea's father would look after the building and anchor the project. The building would be used for storing rice, training women to sew, a place for providing extra education for local children as well as a site for Fellowship activities on Sunday.

Kunthea made his father angry that year by suggesting he sell his cows, and give me the money. He asked why he should do that when I was clearly better off than them. 'Because she must spend her money on a tractor for our land', he replied. He is a special boy. He would always ring me to see if I was okay. I started to think about how I could make a difference in his life.

It was agreed that I would take more responsibility for Kunthea's future and be his adopted mother. His parents were very happy with this. I suggested he come and live at KSL when he was in Grade 10. This would give him the responsibility of looking after the place at night, together with another student. So I have an adopted son! He still calls me mum and goes back most weekends to his parents and will probably become a Khmer teacher at our school if he wants to.

'Yumareac!'

When we started our project in Prek Ho, we met Phi Sa Em (our friend from Cha Huoy times) again and she was interested in what we were doing to help the poor. She told us of some families from her village of Stung Chriw that were almost on deaths door and asked if we could help. The husband in the first family fetched morning glory from a pond and sold it to buy some food for his wife and 2 children. The wife had AIDS and spent all day immobilized on her bed. The children didn't go to school.

We visited her and could see she was only just hanging to life. Her skin had blotches typical of HIV-AIDS sufferers and she barely knew we were there. We prayed for her. By the time we had returned home we heard she has passed away.

We helped arrange a funeral and continued to help the husband look after his children for a further 6 months, through providing rice and some small amounts of money. After 6 months he too passed away with complications from AIDS. The children were now passed to grandparents to look after.

The 'coincidence' that people we worked with kept dying did not go unnoticed by some people in the village. Reflecting a black sense of humour, and a lack of knowledge about AIDS, they called us 'yumareac', which translates roughly as a demon guarding those departed souls with bad karma, and so keeping them out of heaven. Not a flattering label!

Wantha graduated as a doctor in 1986 and spent most of her professional life as a doctor working to combat the AIDS epidemic in Cambodia.

I learnt a lot about this from her, as well as from my role in the hospital. I saw how, in so many ways, AIDS is a disease of the poor. With a lack of employment opportunities the poor are more vulnerable to risky activities, in pursuit of income. They are less likely to be informed about how to protect themselves, and less able to access health services for HIV or other sexually transmitted infections if they succumb.

This trap is further compounded by social norms and power disparities, which marginalize women. A young woman is not expected to be knowledgeable about sexual matters, and certainly not to suggest or insist on use of condoms. Low literacy, poor education and an inability to insist on safe sex, make it less likely she can remain uninfected.

For men who are forced away from home for work, especially in the armed forces, several factors conspire to make it more likely that unsafe sex will occur. The culture of masculinity and risk taking, having a disposable income, excessive alcohol consumption and feelings of invulnerability and anonymity by being away from home, create a perfect storm for infections like HIV-AIDS to take hold. And when they return home they bring it with them to their wives and partners.

In Prek Ho we ran two educational sessions for such vulnerable women and the local village leader attended. We explained about condoms and safe sex, and the dangers of multiple partners. The audience were mostly embarrassed when we talked about these things but those who saw or knew the AIDS victims in their final days, men and women alike, were attentive. Outreach programs to entertainment workers - girls in karaoke bars, massage parlours as well as brothels – are also making indents into the problem. Now drug users and homosexual men, marginalized or shunned groups, are most at risk.

ABOUT THE AUTHORS

Addheka continues to work in the Khmer School of Language (KSL) in Phnom Penh, and administers to the Aid Projects of Mercy on her weekends, driving all over the country. She lives in the capital with her sister Wantha. Addheka can be contacted at laddha88@yahoo.com

Jim works at Curtin University in Perth and has been a teacher for 30 years. He can be contacted at jimpollock19@gmail.com

Lightning Source UK Ltd.
Milton Keynes UK
UKHW040612211218
334380UK00001B/38/P